Derwent Information is the world's leading patent and scientific information provider and has been helping companies stay ahead of the competition for 50 years.

Our parent company, The Thomson Corporation, is a highly focused e-information and solutions company that serves the global business and professional marketplace. Derwent is part of Thomson Scientific; a leading provider of value-added databases and software tools that enable the scientific research community to access and manage published materials.

With our unique and unrivalled portfolio of information and research products, including our flagship product, the *Derwent World Patents Index*®, Derwent has become the first port of call for all the major users of patent information. Our customer base spans the chemical, pharmaceutical, biotechnology and engineering sectors, as well as legal, financial and academic sectors, research libraries and national patent organisations – worldwide.

DERWENT
™
THOMSON SCIENTIFIC

Contents

Foreword
The Internet and intellectual property
Francis Gurry
Assistant Director General
World Intellectual Property Organisation (WIPO)

The Internet is the most powerful instrument yet developed for distributing throughout the world what has become known simply as 'content'. As such, its purpose is entirely compatible with, and complementary to, the objectives of the intellectual property (IP) system which, since the beginning, have been directed at encouraging the creation and the availability of new inventions and cultural works.

· Despite this compatibility of underlying purpose, however, the Internet presents some radical challenges to the historical system of IP protection. In fact, the Internet is challenging every dimension of that system, and most notably in the following areas.

    (i)   *Space:* the economic phenomenon of global markets, combined with the technological phenomenon of the borderless medium of the Internet, is straining the territorial basis of the IP system, which envisages a world divided into separate physical jurisdictions from which intellectual property rights emanate and to which they are limited.

(ii) *Time:* the speed of both technical and business developments in the digital economy is throwing up new issues at a rate which the slow and laborious processes of multilateral negotiations and treaty-making finds difficult, if not impossible, to accommodate.

(iii) *Substance:* new values have emerged on the Internet, such as the open code movement, and new tensions with IP protection are apparent, such as the tension between measuring the use of intellectual property (for example, music) and protecting privacy.

(iv) *Institutions:* the dominant political message in respect of electronic commerce has been that the private sector should lead. How does this translate into IP policy, where the public sector has always established the framework?

(v) *Access:* the Internet has made access to cultural creations easier and cheaper, but only for a limited portion of the world's population. How will the digital divide be narrowed in order to broaden participation in the benefits that the Internet offers?

These challenges are fundamental and the viability of IP will depend on its capacity to respond to them. IP has proven resilient to new technologies in the past: copyright has been successfully adapted from print to photography, sound recordings, cinematography and computer software.

The aim now must be for IP to find a means of continuing to return value to creators, while harnessing the power of the Internet to distribute creations. The early signs indicate that this aim will be met through a combination of technological and legal protection.

The technological measures of protection, such as encryption, are being developed and deployed by the private sector, while the legal measures, such as rules prohibiting the circumvention of technological measures of protection, are part of the evolving legal framework contained in legislative instruments, such as the 1996 WIPO Copyright Treaty and WIPO Performances and Phonograms Treaty.

The present book is a most welcome contribution to the analysis and discussion of the complex challenges that the Internet is presenting for intellectual property.

Introduction

The impact that the Internet is having on business is inescapable, and the commercial consequences of having to operate in the knowledge economy – of which the Internet is an integral part – are now a source of constant deliberation by companies around the globe.

To date, the focus of these deliberations has primarily been on how traditional business processes need to be adapted to the web. Yet while intellectual property (IP) is one of the core assets of the knowledge economy, the implications of the Internet for IP have until recently tended to be neglected.

There is no doubt that traditional IP and the web are on a collision course. IP owners would be mistaken to assume that the courts will be able to easily resolve the disputes that are beginning to arise from this conflict. Just consider the following incidents.

- In September 1999, Amazon.com announced that it had a US patent on its 1-Click shopping process. In response, web users immediately organised petitions of protest and a boycott of the online retailer. Amazon.com's CEO, Jeff

Bezos, subsequently published an open letter stating that the current patent laws appear to be at odds with the principles of the web.

- In November 1999, a Swiss-based art group calling itself etoy.com was forced to close down its web site when online retailing giant eToys won a preliminary injunction against the use of the domain name in a California State Court. Again, the web community immediately organised a boycott against eToys, and called for 'digital riots' and 'virtual sit-ins' aimed at crashing the retailer's web servers. A month later the online retailer agreed to drop its trademark protection case against the art group.

- In July 2000, US Federal Judge Marilyn Patel ordered the web music swapping service, Napster – used by 28 million people – to block its users from trading copyrighted songs via its web site. Within hours of the ruling, millions of Napster users had migrated to the many alternative services. Several days later an appeals court agreed to a stay of execution on the closure. Then in November came the startling announcement from Bertelsmann, one of the companies suing the file-swapping service, that it would drop its lawsuit if Napster created a charged-for 'membership-based service'. It also said it planned to invest in Napster itself.

- In August 2000, US District Judge Lewis Kaplan outlawed the *linking* to web sites that offered internet users access to a DVD decryption utility called Decode Content Scrambling System (DeCSS). The online publication at the centre of the controversy – *2600* – sidestepped the ban by replacing the hypertext links with the text of the URLs concerned, thus allowing users to simply cut and paste the addresses into their web browsers, rather than clicking on a link. Subsequently *2600* also inserted a direct link to the Disney site and advised users to search for the offending piracy tool using the Disney search engine. This mischievously demonstrated that one of the media companies, which had sued *2600* was itself unwittingly providing the links that the court had outlawed.

These are just four examples of the kind of challenges to IP posed by the Internet. Not surprisingly, incidents like these are sparking a heated debate in the US about the role of traditional IP – notably copyright, patents and trademarks – in a web economy. This debate is starting to exercise European minds too.

On one side, traditionalists argue that the Internet does not change anything fundamental, and that the web will eventually be absorbed by the IP system. On the other, web enthusiasts insist that the nature of the web (above all its digital, networked, and global characteristics) makes traditional IP irrelevant, or at least unenforceable.

Whoever is right – and whatever the future holds – these issues are crucial to all of us, especially governments, companies, and lawyers.

Governments are responding to the digital age with new legislation but in some instances this is inflaming the problem. Companies and consumers are threatened with the prospect of their web development slowing to a crawl, hindered by a plague of lawsuits. Companies may then be forced to hold back from migrating their businesses into cyber-space.

At the same time, traditional companies could face the threat of their existing business models collapsing, without the comfort of being able to replace them with new business models. In addition 'new economy' companies could find their energies, and budgets, drained by legal disputes.

Most worryingly, many businesses appear unaware of the imminence, or the extent, of the threat they face. In August 2000, the web magazine *Red Herring* conducted a survey of film and television producers, and 75% of those questioned were confident that copyright can be protected on the Internet, despite the fact that foolproof digital rights management systems are in their infancy and films are already being swapped over the web without regard for copyright laws.

"As the broadband roll-out accelerates," warned Rafe Needleman, editor of *Red Herring*, "the film industry is going to get Napsterized. Of course, it will try to shut this technology down – even though that's not really possible."

These developments look like good news for lawyers, whose business can be expected to grow as a result. But any increase in revenues could prove short-lived if clients conclude that the law cannot adequately resolve the issues.

Everyone affected must give much more thought to the issues the web raises for IP and co-operate to find solutions that are workable and equitable. This book hopes to kick-start that process.

Chapter One
All change or *plus ça change?*
By Richard Poynder

One of the most compelling questions of our times is the extent to which the web will transform our lives. Does it fundamentally alter the social and economic laws that seemed immutable; or does it merely change some of the ways in which we operate our businesses, communicate with each other, and organise our lives?

The polarisation of investor sentiment between 'old economy' companies (as represented by the Dow Jones Index) and 'new economy' companies (traded on NASDAQ) reflects that degree of uncertainty, as do the dichotomised discussions about the web taking place every day in newspapers, on television and on the web.

The majority of this discussion tends to focus around questions of pornography, work patterns, business models, management style and investment choice, but there is a less obvious, although equally important, debate under way about the role of traditional intellectual property (IP) in the new economy.

Until now, much of this discussion has taken place amongst lawyers and IP specialists, mainly in the US, but, increasingly, the topic is attracting the attention of governments, regulators, and even the main-stream media. Meanwhile, the debate is also spreading and becoming as controversial a topic in Europe and Asia as it is in the US.

It is a discussion that inspires heated exchanges from opposing camps – not to mention costly litigation! On the one hand there are those who, like Victor Siber, former head of IP at IBM and now with New York lawyers Clifford Chance Rogers & Wells, argue that the web has changed very little with regard to IP rights.

On the other hand, internet organisations, such as the Electronic Frontier Foundation (EFF) and the World Wide Web Consortium (W3C) along with supporters of the free and open source software movements, like Richard Stallman (founder of the free software move-ment) and Tim O'Reilly (open source activist and founder of O'Reilly & Associates), argue that traditional views of IP are in conflict with web development.

So what is specific about the web that it has triggered this debate? And what are the implications of the changes it introduces?

What's new?

Digital copying, and the ability to generate endless replicas without loss of quality is not new of course. What is new is that the web has made it possible to replicate – and then distribute – multiple copies of copyrighted material to any number of people around the world with the click of a mouse. The web, in short, exemplifies the 'network effect' – if you are the only one with an internet connection, it isn't worth very much since there are no others to email to or any web sites to visit. As the network expands, and friends, family and business contacts all get connected, that connection becomes exponentially more valuable. As Kevin Kelly, editor-at-large of *Wired* magazine, points out: "Mathematics says the sum value of a network increases as the square of the number of members."

The implication of this for owners of IP is that their copyrighted mate-rials, including software, music, pictures and – once broadband becomes widely available – whole movies, can be flawlessly pirated at will. As more and more people are wired to the Internet, so the threat of this piracy grows rapidly.

Clearly this phenomenon has considerable implications for copyright.

The knowledge economy

Related to the rise of the web, and linked in a chicken-and-egg relationship, is the knowledge, or 'new' economy. While the web is in many ways the product of the knowledge economy, it is at the same time a very powerful facilitator of it.

One implication of the knowledge economy is that it is increasing the value that companies, organisations and individuals attach to the knowledge, or intellectual assets, that they create or acquire. Today, ideas are increasingly viewed as a company's most important assets. As Fred Warshofsky, author of *The Patent Wars*, states: "The new technologies, new processes, and new products that constitute IP now form the economic bedrock of international trade and national wealth. Human creativity in the form of ideas, innovations, and inventions has replaced gold, colonies, and raw materials as the new wealth of nations."

As a result, companies are becoming far more focused on protecting their ideas and their innovations and they are turning to IP laws in order to do this. We are, therefore, seeing much greater interest in copyright and trademarks. More controversially, the web has sparked an arms race of patenting activity as companies flood patent offices with applications to patent web-based technologies and business methods.

The triumph of non-rivalrous consumption and open source software?

The ease with which digital content can be distributed on the web has also stimulated growing interest in 'non-rivalrous consumption'. This, in turn, has raised questions about the role of traditional IP in the new economy, with some concluding that IP is inappropriate or irrelevant on the web.

What do we mean by non-rivalrous consumption? It is best understood by comparing it with the way in which we 'consume' property. "When property law gave me the exclusive right to use my house, there was a very good reason for it," explains Lawrence Lessig in his recent book, *Code and Other Laws of Cyberspace.* "If you used my house while I did, I would have less to use. When the law gives me exclusive right to my apple, that too makes sense. If you eat my apple, then I cannot."

By contrast, he continues, "If you 'take' my idea, I still have it. If I tell you an idea, you have not deprived me of it. An unavoidable feature of intellectual property is that its consumption, as the economists like to put it, is 'non-rivalrous'. Your consumption does not lessen mine. If I write a song, you can sing it without making it impossible for me to sing it. If I write a book, you can read it without disabling me from reading it. Ideas, at their core, can be *shared* with no reduction in the amount the 'owner' can consume. This difference is fundamental."

This distinction lies at the heart of the free and open source software movements, which are based on the principle that software development is not about proprietary ownership, but a joint project for the common good. The benefit of this approach, argue open source advocates, is that by making the source code openly available anyone can improve and build on the core program and, in so doing, vastly speed up development times, and ensure a more bug-free product (more eyes mean a better chance of fixing mistakes and rooting out bugs).

One step beyond this lies free software, which is available for reuse and copying without licensing. "Free software is software that everybody is free to copy or modify," explains Richard Stallman. "It becomes free software because the author has authorised copying or modification. Free software is an example of developing material without obstructing its use and its users."

The fact that the web exemplifies the notion of non-rivalrous consumption so successfully has important commercial implications for all copyright owners, argues Esther Dyson, new economy thinker and chairman of the Internet Corporation for Assigned Names and Numbers (ICANN). "The net poses interesting challenges for owners/creators/sellers and for users of intellectual property," she says in her newsletter, *Release 1.0.* "Because it allows for costless copying of content, it dramatically changes the economics of content." We shall return to this point.

The co-operative ethos that has reigned in cyberspace has important implications for the patent system too, and brings the current patent arms race into direct conflict with those who point out that the Internet was built not on exclusive ownership of the technology, but through mutual sharing of techniques and methods.

As Tim O'Reilly argued in an e-mail to Amazon.com CEO, Jeff Bezos, when hearing that Amazon had been granted a patent on 1-Click shopping: "The web has grown so rapidly because it has been an open platform for experimentation and innovation. It broke us loose from the single-vendor stranglehold that Microsoft has had on much of the software industry." However, he added "Once the web becomes fenced in by competing patents and other attempts to make this glorious open playing field into a proprietary wasteland, the springs of further innovation will dry up."

The boundaries expand

The knowledge economy, and the rash of e-commerce patents that Tim O'Reilly finds so objectionable, is also testing the boundaries of IP law. Following two important court rulings, the patenting landscape in the US has changed dramatically. Firstly, a US Supreme Court decision in 1981 – *Diamond v. Diehr* – opened the door to the patenting of software, which until then had only been protected by copyright laws. Subsequently, in 1998, the US Court of Appeals of the Federal Circuit (CAFC) ruled that business methods could also be patented – *State Street Bank & Trust Co v. Signature Financial Group Inc.*

Taken together these two decisions have unleashed a flood of controversial internet patents. In effect, argue critics, they have made it possible to take any known business method from the real world, build the process in software, apply that process to the Internet, and then obtain a patent on it.

Currently, another controversial e-commerce patent is unleashed on the world practically every week. The list of most contentious patents includes British Telecom's patent on hyperlinking, Amazon.com's patent on 1-Click shopping, Open Market's patent on web shopping trolleys, Priceline.com's patent on name-your-price auctions, and Sightsound.com's patent on downloading music over the web. As the web moves into the mobile market, a further rash of controversial patents is starting to flood the marketplace, most notably a claim by GeoWorks that is has a patent on Wireless Application Protocol (WAP) itself.

Clearly this phenomenon can be expected to have a considerable impact on patents and the patent system and we cannot expect this to remain a US-only issue. Not only are other countries and regions, including the EU, reviewing the possibility of enabling the patenting of software but, as we shall discover, a US patent can have a wider impact than in the US alone.

New territories to colonise

The web is also a new frontier. As companies rush to carve out a presence in cyberspace an unprecedented land grab is under way to migrate corporate brands and trademarks into the virtual new world of cyberspace. This involves companies acquiring desired domain names – even where previously assigned to others – by recourse to trademark laws. While this practice has attracted the criticism of those who believe that a more equitable arrangement would be to operate an exclusively 'first-come, first-served' system, companies argue that they have a legitimate right to protect their IP on the web.

Today, with increasing support from the courts, and initiatives from international organisations like the World Intellectual Property Organisation (WIPO), the so-called cyber-squatters are under considerable pressure. However, with ICANN planning to introduce a host of new top level domain names, this conflict could easily escalate in the short-term.

Additionally, with national laws wrestling to make sense of the global nature of the network, the conflicts and uncertainties go beyond the activities of unscrupulous cyber-squatters. US companies, for instance, often find themselves at loggerheads with European companies, organisations or individuals, particularly where they trade under the same name in different legal jurisdictions.

This was amply demonstrated in 1999 when eToys.com, a leading US-based e-commerce site, sued a group of Swiss artists using the domain name etoy.com for trademark infringement, complaining that their customers were accidentally going to the wrong site and being exposed to violent images and profanity. Interestingly, after a Los Angeles Court issued a preliminary injunction ordering the artists to stop using the domain name www.etoy.com, eToys.com became the target for a barrage of criticism from the web community which eventually persuaded the company to drop its lawsuit.

In another striking example of corporate determination to 'own' all its IP assets in cyberspace, UK-based Road Tech won a court case against its rival, Mandata, by arguing that the use of Road Tech's Roadrunner trademark in the invisible meta-tags in Mandata's web pages was an infringement. (Meta-tags provide indexing details of web sites that are visible only to search engines, and are valuable ways of boosting a site's ranking in web searches.) The decision cost Mandata in the region of £80,000.

The heart of the debate

At the heart of this debate lies a simple question: is traditional IP in the knowledge economy merely litter from a past industrial age, or are those ideas, innovations, and inventions that Warshofsky describes as the "economic bedrock of international trade and national wealth" in need of exactly the same protection on the web as they have everywhere else?

Sitting on one side of the table is the web community, which argues that the web is – and should be – viewed as radically different when it comes to IP. Their fear is that we are currently witnessing the creeping privatisation of the core assets of the web and the knowledge economy. "There has been a fundamental paradigm shift," suggests writer Seth Shulman in his book, *Owning the Future*. "In the rush to stake claims in the knowledge economy, we risk auctioning off our technological and cultural heritage."

Web culture also assumes that, on the Internet, 'information wants to be free' and that cyberspace should be non-commercial, unregulated, uncensored and self-regulating. Add to this the ethos of the open source movement, which is committed to the co-operative development of the Internet, and you have the core of the conflict being played out over IP and the web today.

"Patents such as yours are the first step in vitiating the web," wrote Tim O'Reilly to Jeff Bezos, "in raising the barriers to entry not just for your competitors, but for the technological innovators who might otherwise come up with great new ideas that you could put to use in your business."

On the other side of the table sit the corporations, the lawyers and, increasingly, national governments. They argue that the web is no different to any other aspect of human society, or commerce, and as such needs to be regulated and legislated for in the same way. For the establishment, traditional IP laws are as relevant on the web as off the web. At most, they say, there might be a need for some fine-tuning of current laws, and IP systems, to fit the new medium.

"The detractors of IP rights have been crying doomsday for as long as I can recall but the interesting thing is that doomsday never comes," argues Clifford Chance's Victor Siber. "The world has never seen such a rapid and pervasive growth of technology and business based on digital information. If patents and copyrights have gotten in the way of this advance, it most certainly is not evident."

Bob Hart, chairman of the Computer Technology Committee of the UK's Chartered Institute of Patent Agents (CIPA), agrees: "Activity on the web is little different to activity anywhere else. It has always been very difficult in some areas to establish infringement, and it is difficult with the web. But the only new problem that the web introduces is the territoriality of patents and trademarks. That is just an issue that needs to be worked out by international agreement."

Two responses

Faced with the anarchic tendencies of the web, the establishment has taken a two-pronged approach to protecting IP on the web: new laws and new technology.

To date the primary focus of legislators has been to extend and adapt copyright protection. In the US this has taken the form of the Digital Millennium Copyright Act (DMCA) of 1998. The European response is coming in the shape of the proposed EU Copyright Directive.

Additionally, with the aim of protecting trademarks on the web, US Congress passed the Anti Cyber-Squatting Consumer Protection Act in 1999, which makes it possible to fine cyber-squatters up to $100,000.

International organisations like WIPO have also been active. In fact, the new copyright legislation in the US and Europe came about as a result of the WIPO Copyright Treaty, and the WIPO Performances and Phonograms Treaty. These same treaties should lead to the introduction of similar copyright legislation in a number of other nations.

In 1999, WIPO also introduced the Uniform Domain Name Dispute Resolution Policy (UDRP), designed to settle conflicts over trademarks on the Internet and, in July 2000, WIPO announced a further initiative to extend its activities into bad faith domain name registrations.

In respect of patent laws, there has been little in the way of new legislation but, as we have seen, the courts have brought about very considerable changes to the patent system in the US; changes which are now reverberating around the world.

In addition, the World Trade Organisation (WTO) has for a number of years been actively trying to harmonise patent laws around the world, with a view to better adapting them to the knowledge economy. This is mainly through the Trade-Related Aspects of Intellectual Property Rights (TRIPs) initiative, which was signed in 1995 and is having some impact on the global patent environment.

Fighting fire with fire

Parallel with developments in the law, technology companies have been busy developing new software tools to try and prevent infringement on the web. A growing number of digital rights management systems (DRMs) are becoming available, including systems that utilise electronic keys, date, time and 'first-use' stamps, as well as encryption systems and audit trails.

Amongst those now available for uniquely identifying and protecting copyrighted content are InterTrust's MetaTrust Utility, Microsoft's Media Player and Xerox's ContentGuard. In 1999, ContentGuard was spun off as a separate company, partly funded by Microsoft, and tasked with developing a DRM standard, XrML (eXtensible rights Markup Language). The aim is to enable interoperability across different DRM systems, and Microsoft Reader, which is a new software product for displaying e-Books, is the first product to incorporate the new technology.

Likewise, with the intention of protecting music on the web, Digital Media on Demand, a Boston start-up, has created an encryption system that enables artists to encode and track online files. It includes watermarks – in which content in audio files is stamped with new data that is inaudible to the human ear – that trace the file back to the artist who uploaded it and to the consumer who downloaded it. The moment the user acquires a piece of content, the keys are generated and the file is encrypted based on those dynamic keys.

There are also a number of industry initiatives, including the Secure Digital Music Initiative (SDMI). Established in 1999, this encompasses 160 music, technology, hardware and software companies. The aim is to develop a secure, open standard for providing digital rights management for musicians and allow music companies to charge for music on the Internet.

New laws: slow and brutal

The first problem confronting legislators is that web technology moves so fast that new laws are in danger of being out-of-date by the time they enter the statute book. Some commentators argue that the DMCA is already out-moded having, amongst other things, failed to anticipate the revolutionary nature of new music swapping services that have arisen on the web, such as Napster.

Secondly, there are concerns that, in introducing the new legislation, governments are shifting the balance of equity too far in the direction of rights owners, and away from the rights of the public. Critics claim that the DMCA acts against the long-held tradition of 'fair use' – the right of a member of the public to use copyrighted material, regardless of the wishes of the owner of that material.

Similar criticism has been made by the UK Consumers' Association (CA) of the EU Copyright Directive. The CA argues that the Directive fails to "distinguish between pirates and consumers." For example, it adds, it could lead to the outlawing of the current 'fair use' provision allowing consumers to record TV programmes for later viewing. "We think it should distinguish between someone who wants to pirate a video and someone who just wants to catch an episode of their favourite soap," says the CA.

Likewise, the DMCA's outlawing of 'anti-circumvention' encryption systems has had some unexpected consequences. This is best exemplified by a legal dispute that saw the EFF lined up against the Motion

Picture Association of America (MPAA). At issue was a software utility, Decode Content Scrambling System (DeCSS), developed to disable the encryption system used on DVDs, and the online magazine, *2600*, was sued for promoting the software.

While the MPAA argued that the DMCA outlawed any technology intended to circumvent systems designed to protect copyrighted material, the EFF pointed out that without such a utility it would be impossible for users to watch DVDs they already own on the Linux operating system. If the courts outlaw DeCSS, argued the EFF's John Gilmore, "it will become illegal to build open source products that can operate and/or compete with proprietary ones for displaying copyright material."

Speaking to the *New York Times* at the time of the trial Yochai Benker, a law professor and internet expert at New York University, commented: "Up until now, there has been no general right to control the reading of a book or to control access to a work. This case is a well-focused presentation of the question of whether or not the DMCA created a new right to control access to a work if the work is encoded and encrypted in digital media." In the event, the judge ruled against *2600* but the case has been appealed.

In any case, critics point out, if the new laws are seen to be unfair people will simply ignore them, in the same way as they tend to ignore speed limits they believe to be impractical.

National laws vis-à-vis global network

An additional problem faced by current attempts at legislating for the protection of web-based IP is that it inevitably means trying to solve international problems with the limited powers provided by national laws.

As WIPO points out on its web site: "In a fundamental respect, the international character of electronic commerce raises questions for the ature of traditional legal systems in general, and IP law in particular. oth are based on notions of sovereignty and territoriality. The

Internet, in contrast, like the movement of weather within the global climate, largely ignores distinctions based on territorial borders. Instead, infrastructure, code and language have thus far had a greater bearing on the reach of its currents."

As we have seen, this is a real problem for companies wishing to exert their trademark rights, which are territorial, in order to obtain domain names, which are, of necessity, international in scope.

For patent owners the problems are similarly complex. Quite apart from the problems posed by nations disagreeing on what is and is not patentable, there are the thorny issues of jurisdiction. The question for a company operating around web patents would be: "If I have a browser that is logged into a European server, is the browser subject to European patents, US patents or both? Obviously if a server is operating on US soil, that server is subject to US patents. It becomes even more complicated if I have a browser in Europe attached to a server in Japan, and they happen to be transiting a US network."

Enforcement also poses considerable difficulties, points out Alan Fisch, a prominent attorney with Howrey Simon Arnold & White in Washington DC. "Even if every patent authority in the world agreed on what was patentable, there would still remain enforcement hurdles. Nations lack agreement as to whether it is permissible for one of their patents to be enforced against an infringer whose system is part-located or operating outside their respective border."

Commissioner of the US Patent and Trademark Office (USPTO), Todd Q Dickinson, agrees that the "complexity of having territorial patenting systems" is a hurdle. The solution, he says, "is a cheap, simple and effective worldwide patent system."

This is an aim of international organisations like WIPO and the WTO, which are both committed to increasing harmonisation of IP laws. Clearly, however, this is not going to happen overnight and, given the speed of development on the Internet, this suggests we can see a worrying period of uncertainty ahead.

Winning the technology war

Those seeking to assert traditional IP rights on the web by means of technology also face a number of hurdles, not least that of being able to develop anti-piracy solutions that are not immediately circumvented by hackers, and others without respect for IP rights.

The fragility of today's technological padlocks should not be overlooked. When it was launched, the Sega Dreamcast games console was said to be the most secure digital entertainment system on the market. Within months a group of hackers calling itself 'Utopia' had broken through its copyright protections and released a set of copied games online – along with a software program that could trick the Dreamcast hardware into playing the games without any modifications to the hardware itself.

Moreover, there must be concern that those industry groups focused on creating new security standards simply cannot operate at the speed required to keep ahead of the pirates and hackers. Although the SDMI produced an early Phase I security outline for portable devices, for instance, practical developments have been slow to arrive.

In fact, when interviewed by *Wired's* online news service in July 2000, the head of SDMI, Leonardo Chiariglione, was worryingly phlegmatic. "There is no reason that because technology moves fast, you shouldn't apply security," he said. "The house where my grandfather lived had ridiculously weak padlocks. My house has more sophisticated padlocks. So there is no reason that because it is easy for a thief to enter a house, not to put a padlock. The same goes for SDMI."

The threat of P2P

Perhaps the greatest threat from technology for IP owners today, however, is the recent development of open source programs designed to re-introduce the unregulated structure that was the norm in the early days of the Internet. The aim is to re-assert the original counter-cultural ethos that believes the network should be free, non-commercial, unregulated, uncensored and self-regulating.

Specifically, a new generation of 'peer-to-peer' (P2P) services, including Gnutella and Freenet, have begun to proliferate. By using a decentralised and distributed architecture (with no central server) these new services are able to circumvent the regulated public internet, and the law, and guarantee users anonymity. As the founder of Freenet, Ian Clarke, puts it: "There is no person, computer, or organisation in control of Freenet or essential in its operation."

Moreover, he added, it has been specifically designed to automatically spread itself to other nodes when information is under attack by an entity attempting to enforce a copyright. And since, unlike Napster, Freenet isn't a company, it cannot be sued by rights owners.

That these services are a direct threat to IP cannot be doubted. When asked to comment on the potential of Freenet to allow copyright theft, Ian Clarke commented to online news service, *etown.com*: "Stealing implies that you're dealing with property. I disagree with people who say information is the same as other forms of property. I'm not so sure you can treat information like real estate or gold."

In effect, these new services are building an anonymous and unregulated layer on top of the public internet, thus making it doubly difficult for IP owners to enforce their rights. Marc Andreesen, creator of the Netscape browser, has called these new services the most important development since the invention of the browser.

Moreover it is not renegade open source programmers like Ian Clarke alone that are creating this new anonymity. In June 2000, AT&T Labs announced that it had developed a new system, called Publius, which allows users to surf the web anonymously. Designed primarily to overcome censorship, the new system clearly has implications for copyright and other forms of IP, as it would make it hard to trace an original transaction, and the sender can break data files into many pieces and send them via a number of different servers.

The business model conundrum

So will the technology battle be lost, or is it simply that the establishment has yet to develop the necessary weapons with which to fight back? Will the law prove unable to stamp out wholesale copyright infringement, or will it again find a satisfactory balance between the rights of IP owners and the public? Will it succeed in eradicating cyber-squatting, or continue to struggle to juggle the competing demands of trademark laws and the web?

Likewise, will the growing outcry against the patenting of web technologies become so strident that governments will feel obliged to intervene, or will the web be successfully absorbed by the patent system?

Today we cannot know the answers to these questions. There are, however, a growing number of 'independent' thinkers who argue that the web is different and special when it comes to IP. Proponents of this view argue that, rather than fighting a war they may not win, companies would be far better finding new business models that fit better with the web economy.

What rights owners need to understand on the web is the difference between IP, intellectual value and market value, says Esther Dyson. "The problem for providers of intellectual property is that although under law they can control the pricing of their own products, they will operate in an increasingly competitive marketplace, where much intellectual property is distributed free and the number of providers is exploding."

Content providers are already having to face this reality. With so many information sites now offering free content, people are not generally prepared to pay for information on the web today – except for very powerful branded products like the *Wall Street Journal*. Currently, therefore, the dominant business model for publishers on the web involves giving content away, and seeking to earn revenues from other sources, such as advertising. "The likely best defence for content providers is to exploit the situation," says Esther Dyson. "To distribute intellectual property free in order to sell services and relationships."

Even that staunch bastion of the traditional IP system, the music industry, is starting to have doubts. In July 2000, Jimmy Lovine, head of Seagram's online venture Farmclub.com, commented to the *Los Angeles Times*: "The [music] industry is in protection overdrive. The only reason MP3.com and Napster exist is because the record industry never did anything in this space." He added: "I'm all for protecting music. But we can't wait until we invent the digital padlock. That could take 20 years. We don't have 20 years. We need to move now."

It is, after all, the open source model that enabled Linus Torvalds, the original author of the Linux operating system, to make his software so successful. By making the source code freely available on the web, and inviting thousands of freelance programmers to help in its development, Torvalds has seen Linux become a considerable thorn in the side of Microsoft. Arguably, it has also changed the agenda for software development forever.

Likewise, owners of e-commerce patents may find that the cost of enforcing – in terms of negative PR and lost business – patents may eventually outweigh the benefits. As one technology and IP expert commented on hearing about the BT hyperlink patent: "The commercial damage and unpopularity, which BT would bring on its head if it tried to enforce this patent, would be incalculable."

Interestingly, as Esther Dyson suggests, the logic of the new business model implicit in the open source movement is not that IP is irrelevant or worthless, but that its value changes. In the knowledge economy, ironically, IP may eventually prove to have less, not more, value than previously.

"Knowledge is merging so much over the world that ownership is going to be much, much more difficult to establish," argues PricewaterhouseCoopers' Gordon Petrash. "Ultimately – maybe in fifty years or a hundred years, but ultimately – the knowledge that is developed, and the value that is derived from it, will be based on who can use it the quickest and the best, not on who owns it. Besides, how do you own something that, as soon as you think of it, it goes to zillions of people over the Internet? How do you own something that is continuously being built on, talked about, improved, discussed?"

Traditionalists, however, remain sceptical. "Of course there is a small band of elite snobs who have managed to market their services by giving their IP away," says Clifford Chance's Victor Siber. "That is their choice. But to impose their approach on the rest of the world is simply wrong."

Adds the Chartered Institute of Patent Agent's Bob Hart: "If you make your copyrighted material freely available on the web then you are effectively freely licensing the rights you have. That is up to you. But this content isn't free, it is freely licensed. And for those who don't want to freely licence their material, but want remuneration for it, it is vital that copyright remains available."

Richard Poynder interviews Gordon Petrash, Partner, Competency Leader Intellectual Asset Management Practice, at PricewaterhouseCoopers

Q: Does the web present traditional IP with a serious problem?

A: *The situation has still to be defined, so the serious problem is the unknown. What we have is a collision occurring. People who are innovative and inventive, for example patenting things because they have good ideas, while on the other side we have the internet culture, which believes in keeping things open and free.*

Q: This polarisation lies at the heart of the debate?

A: *Right. And the other piece is the rules. We are finding that governments and the regulators cannot move as quickly as the market, so the rules are constantly trying to keep up.*

Q: Is there a danger that these new rules could make matters worse? It is said, for instance, that the US Digital Millennium Copyright Act tilts the balance too far in the favour of rights owners, and against the interests of the public. The EU Copyright Directive has attracted similar criticism?

A: *That could be the case, but it is too soon to say. One of the dilemmas we have with IP law is that when we make these decisions we don't know what the impact will be two or three years down the road.*

Q: You don't agree with those who argue that traditional IP is irrelevant, or inappropriate, in a web economy?

A: *I agree that there is a lot of frivolousness going on in IP today. Taken to the extreme we could end up where you would never be able to whistle a tune without paying a royalty, or write another song because every chord and note has been patented. Nevertheless, there remain fundamental technologies, processes and ideas that can and should be owned, and have rights attached to them, in order to encourage inventiveness and invɪ ment.*

Q: Nevertheless, desirable or not, confronted with new technologies like Napster and Gnutella it seems that some aspects of IP can no longer be protected in a web economy. Copyright for instance?

A: *Or perhaps we just haven't found the right mechanisms yet. We are, for instance, seeing the development of watermarks that can be placed into music, or software, that cannot be erased. This allows you to trace it back to its origins, no matter how many times it has been copied. So what we currently lack is the necessary technology to keep ownership identified.*

Q: How do you respond to those who argue that, in the scramble to register domain names, large multinational companies are riding roughshod over everyone else's rights through aggressive exploitation of their trademarks in cyberspace?

A: *Anyone can get a domain name, and I have two myself. I think the system is open and clear. If you want to have a name and the dot.com part has gone you can register dot.org or dot.something else.*

Q: Some commentators, notably Seth Shulman, argue that governments will need to restrict what companies can do with their IP, or maybe even nationalise some of it. Is this a likely scenario? One of the proposals in the Microsoft anti-trust case, after all, called for the Windows source code to be put into the public domain.

A: *I don't know. But clearly you can see some political and social forces coming into play. Microsoft has been very successful, and has been able to do certain things using IP – mainly its copyrights and trademarks. But what the Microsoft case shows is that the rules can change, and while IP owners may play by all the rules perfectly correctly, they can still lose if they don't have their eyes on the political and social economic trends.*

Q: So far much of the debate about IP and the web has taken place in the US. Do you see Europe, or perhaps Asia, acting as a brake on the 'frivolousness' to which you referred?

A: *Actually what I think we will see is the development of a global IP system. This will come about through some pain and suffering, but it is just a matter of time and we are going to see global rules converging of necessity.*

Q: And the World Trade Organisation is moving us in this direction through the TRIPs initiative. However, some worry that the dominance of the US in these matters is itself a cause for concern. Amongst other things, it is causing tension between the First World and the Third World.

A: *What is wrong with it being led by the US? Technology is developing so fast that I think it is good that we have a leader that is unrestrained in its look and movement to the future. If we keep stopping to take inventory on who agrees, and who doesn't, it will move very slowly.*

I would also make the case that there are unlimited opportunities for smart people in the Third World. As they become connected to the Internet, and begin to apply themselves to this new world, they will be able to use their creativity and their intelligence to leapfrog some stages that industrialised nations have had to go through – and maybe usurp some of the current advantages industrialised nations have.

Q: So how do you see the debate over IP and the web playing out?

A: *There is a train crash coming. Firstly, there is this perception you referred to that some countries have an unfair advantage, which may cause those nations who feel disadvantaged to just ignore IP all together. Secondly, there is legal interpretation. For instance, the State Street ruling [allowing business methods to be patented] is only 12 months old, and it takes about 18 months for a patent to get through the system. You can be sure there are thousands of people out there right now writing patents that beyond State Street that will come in to play in the next two to five years.*

Q: What are the likely consequences of this?

A: *I don't know how it will end. Some of this IP may ultimately be disallowed. It may also mean that we need some new definitions. Not all patents need to last 20 years, for instance, so we may end up with some patents that exist for just three years, and some ten or fifteen years. In the meantime, however, I am advising all my clients to write as many patents as possible – even though they may eventually be disallowed. I would rather be on the high ground of owning a patent in the next few years rather than on the low ground of trying to fight these patents.*

Q: Whose ultimate responsibility is it to sort this out?

A: *IP is going to have a higher impact in the knowledge economy, so governments will need to have the insight to see the implications of what's happening, to prepare for it, and to have the mechanisms in place to deal with it. And the courts and governmental bodies are going to have to make a determination about what will and will not be allowed in the future.*

Q: Nevertheless, traditional IP still has a role to play on the web?

A: *It does. The IP model remains vital for fundamental innovation and inventiveness. Nobody would invest in this creativity unless they could own it, so do away with IP protection and innovation will fall back.*

Richard Poynder interviews Seth Shulman, author, of *Owning the Future*

Q: Does the web pose a challenge for traditional IP?

A: *It does. The central issue is the tremendous power the web offers for sharing and distributing information, which can be limitlessly replicated over the Internet. The web is also facilitating the knowledge-based economy, in which information and ideas have an increasingly high value. This, in turn, is leading to a very broad privatised approach to the ownership of knowledge.*

Q: Certainly the ease with which music can be shared using services like Napster and Gnutella is posing significant problems for copyright owners.

A: *Right. By providing people with the ability to exchange songs with each other instantaneously over the web, Napster is a wonderful example of the problem faced by IP owners. While one can see that the recording industry has a strong case when it claims that services like Napster are allowing wholesale piracy of copyrighted music, its ability to stop it in the long-term seems to be very, very limited indeed.*

Q: So are copyright owners fighting a losing battle?

A: *Certainly the web's ability to copy, distribute and share knowledge in a dramatic new way is coming right up against traditional ideas about ownership. So anyone clinging on to traditional assumptions is in danger of losing out.*

Q: As opposed to developing new business models. New economy thinkers like Esther Dyson argue that copyright owners will have to give their material away don't they?

A: *I don't go as far as Esther Dyson, who says that many kinds of IP will be so widely distributed that they will have virtually no value and that authors will give their books or articles away, and then charge in a manner akin to the $500 a plate dinner. This overstates it. However, there is no question that we need to find* *new business models. The problem is that it is still too early in the game to know which ones are going to work best.*

Q: The relationship between trademarks and domain names is also an area of conflict. Large companies are accused of unfairly leveraging their trademarks to wrest domain names from others. In turn, they complain that unscrupulous cyber-squatters are blackmailing them into buying what should be theirs by right. What's your view?

A: *While I can see all the pain of the losers, I think trademark issues are of less relevance to the larger topic. The reason is that only one entity can reasonably make use of one domain name or trademark, which is a traditional supply and demand model. The web economy, however, allows what economists refer to as non-rivalrous consumption, where there are no marginal costs attached to replicating and distributing information, and digital products such as software and music, infinitely. This is the key change that is driving the need for new business models.*

Q: E-commerce patents are a third area of controversy today. Is there a problem?

A: *Well, the issues associated with patents today are not unique to the web. We are seeing a very serious problem over what should and should not be patented with the human genome as well. But certainly e-commerce patents are bringing the matter to the fore, as we are seeing some of the worst excesses associated with allowing exclusive ownership of fundamental technologies.*

Q: Which could hinder the development of the web?

A: *Yes. With patents what we need to do is to get our arms around the notion of what I call the infostructure. Like the traditional infrastructure, such as roads etc., we now have the infostructure, and this needs to be regulated and managed in the same way. Because what we are finding, again and again, is that to allow a private entity to own a key piece of the infostructure causes a lot of problems.*

Q: So we need controls over that ownership?

A: *Right, and ownership can change the whole structure of society, so this is a political issue.*

Q: What is the solution?

A: *Actually, we have a lot of experience of ownership, so we should look at how we have handled other kinds of ownership, such as land, for an answer. The best example is that of zoning. Zoning essentially says you can own a piece of land, but it doesn't mean you can build a factory there. Zoning laws uphold community standards of one kind or another, and act as a restraint on the very broad powers of ownership. You can still have ownership, but there are rules and responsibilities that go with it.*

Q: An alternative model is that espoused by the open source movement?

A: *Absolutely. With Linux you have a platform, or operating system, that is available to everyone, and from which they can build their own software products and other value-added services. The analogy is that of having appliances that can all plug into the same wall socket.*

Q: Today the controversy surrounding IP and the web is mainly confined to the US. Do you think North America is moving in the right direction when it comes to resolving the issues?

A: *The US Patent Office is moving dramatically in the wrong direction. Today it effectively has an 'anything goes' approach to patenting. Likewise, court decisions like the State Street case [enabling the patenting of business methods] are definitely taking us in a bad direction. The concept of patenting methods of doing business is ill conceived. The problem is that we are viewing it in a very legalistic way, or in a very limited economic way. Th issues are a matter of public policy. However, so far no policy debate has taken place, so there is a real vacuum.*

Q: I guess that implies government action. Do you think that the Microsoft anti-trust case is relevant to the discussion?

A: *Yes, it is extremely relevant. But the fact of the matter is that anti-trust law is a very 'after-the-fact' weapon, and a bludgeon at that. A more sensible way of dealing with the situation is not to wait until monopolies form, but to avoid handing them out in the first place. Unless we have a thoughtful discussion about what makes sense in the new economy we are going to have a lot more anti-trust cases.*

Q: Clearly the web is a global phenomenon, and the discussion is beginning to move beyond the US. Can you see Europe or Asia reining back on the increasing privatisation of knowledge that you refer to?

A: *The US is pushing this very broad privatised notion of IP matters extremely quickly and forcefully, so it is going to prove a very difficult juggernaut to stop. I don't have much confidence that Europe or Asia will be able to do it, not for a lack of economic strength, but because of the nature of the problem: even while a reasonable debate over these issues might go on, the pressures are immense for companies to protect their bottom line. And in a knowledge-based economy, this means patents and other forms of IP protection.*

Q: In conclusion, traditional IP is inappropriate in a web-enabled knowledge economy, but you don't expect any quick solutions?

A: *Right. The challenge is to recognise that things have changed, and to begin to craft a new compromise, and to develop new business models. The key is to amend the rules to protect our collective vision of the infostructure from the worst excesses of private exploitation, and this can only be done if we recognise that this is a policy issue, and not one that can be left to the courts or the regulators to fix. I am ultimately confident this will happen. It just won't happen easily, or quickly.*

Chapter Two
Copyright in the age of the Internet
By Paul Gosling

The first real copyright law, enacted in 1710 by the British Parliament, was the Statute of Anne. The first US copyright law was passed by Congress in 1790 and, since then, the copyright statutes have been expanded and changed many times. But can a legal framework, established at a time when the printing industry was in its youth, withstand the digital revolution?

Increasingly today books, music, photographs, databases, software, television programmes, films, even fashion designs are whizzed across the world, over the Internet, breaching copyright with apparent impunity.

These are serious issues for copyright owners. Theft of copyright material is already big business. According to the International Intellectual Property Alliance (IIPA), the US copyright industries lost at least $12.4bn in 1998 from piracy in 62 countries that have not fully implemented the World Intellectual Property Organisation (WIPO) treaties. (US income from sale of copyrighted material was valued at $348bn in 1997 – the latest available figures – and is the country's largest export, according to the IIPA.) One estimate suggests that a third of illegal copying is already conducted electronically, mostly over the Internet. The cost of copyright theft is likely to escalate as the technology that facilitates piracy improves, the number of people connected to the Internet rises, and the range of industries under threat increases.

The US is particularly concerned at what it sees as laxness on the part of the EU in policing at least some elements of copyright protection. "We all need to appreciate the massive amount of private copying that goes on in Europe," says Justin Hughes, an attorney and advisor in the US Patent and Trademark Office (USPTO). "It appears that last year [1999] in the Netherlands and Belgium, there were 73 million blank CDs sold – 12 million more than recorded music CDs sold. Now, unless there are lots of karaoke singers who think their voices need to be preserved for posterity, that's a lot of copying of legally protected music. In the end, that translates to a certain number of musicians who are waiting tables instead of making music professionally."

New legislation

In response to the new IP challenge, legislators around the world have updated laws – a process kick-started in 1996 by WIPO, which initiated the WIPO Copyright Treaty and the WIPO Performances and Phonograms Treaty (the internet treaties). With over 50 signatories, the two treaties should produce new copyright legislation worldwide, updating national laws and creating a more uniform, global, legal environment.

An early European Union step towards digital copyright law was its 1996 Directive for the Legal Protection of Databases, and it later revisited the issue through its Electronic Commerce Directive, which clarified and limited internet service provider (ISP) liability.

A further EU directive on copyright in the information society has been agreed in principle by member governments, but may not pass into law until 2001 or later. The proposed directive tries to strike a balance between recognising the rights of consumers in making 'fair copies' –

for example, copying material already owned for personal use – while protecting owners of copyright from commercial exploitation without compensation.

But the courts seem likely to face serious difficulties in interpreting the copyright directive, assuming it passes into law in its draft form. Olswang, a London legal firm specialising in IP, suggests that the directive will remove existing rights for free copying from UK law – whether in digital or paper form – without 'fair compensation'. However, the UK government believes that this principle has been maintained by the directive allowing for member gov~~~~ decide for themselves some details of 'fair use' definition and by the directive's preamble which states that fair compensation ~~~~ ome instances mean no compensation.

Variations in the draft directive's legal application across the EU worries the US. In particular, EU member states may permit private copying as a 'fair use' application but the US believes this would cover any non-commercial use and, in the age of the Internet, could lead to distributing content to millions of people. "This kind of activity is light years from what was originally intended as 'private copying'," says Justin Hughes. "That's the concern with such a broad definition."

In the US, the 1998 Digital Millennium Copyright Act (DMCA) radically updated copyright law. Among its many provisions it amended earlier legislation to enable broadcasting over the Internet and implemented WIPO's internet treaties. In late 1998, the Sono Bono Copyright Term Extension Act became law in the US with the effect of harmonising copyright terms with those applicable in Europe, where copyright lasts for the life of the creator plus 70 years. In the US this had previously been life plus 50 years.

Copyright protection on the web is hampered by different legal frameworks worldwide but particularly in conflicts between the US and EU. The DMCA builds on existing US legislation, which fails to recognise full copyright in broadcast sound records, although it is recognised in the EU. And, according to the British Phonographic Institute (the UK music industry's representative body), the definitions used for 'webcasting' in US and EU legislation vary sufficiently to enable them to mean different things in the two territories.

This reminds us once again that while the Internet is global, law remains national, or at best regional, in scope. In addition, the new legislation does not mean that the scope of copyright law is now entirely clear, or even certain, in either Europe or America. Test cases are needed to fine-tune the law and resolve conflicts of interpretation. As we see below, this is beginning to happen.

Continuing threats

The most widespread theft of copyright over the web has been through software distribution. The relationship between software and copyright has never been a simple one. The US's 1976 copyright law excluded reference to software, but a 1980 amendment made clear that software was protected and could only be copied in specific circumstances, such as for storage in case of disk corruption or computer damage. But, in producing new software, it remains unclear where the line is drawn between copying an expression (breach of copyright) and an idea (not a breach). Producers of software have increasingly turned to patents as an alternative and preferred means of protecting their work.

The web is a major route for the distribution of software in breach of copyright. The Business Software Alliance estimates that in 1999 the worldwide value of trade in pirated software was around $12bn. And this figure may spiral as users exploit file-sharing software to distribute programs.

An even older copyright battlefield is journalism. It is established in Europe and North America, legally and by custom and practice, that freelance journalists (though not staff writers) retain copyright ownership of articles written for publishers – they give up 'first use' only. The exception is where the journalist and publisher agree that 'all rights' or perhaps 'electronic rights' are transferred.

However, many publishers have tried to force journalists to hand over electronic rights, without additional payment, while some publishers have chosen to 'assume' that they own electronic rights or that they can impose ownership of electronic rights without writers' consent. These presumptions were quashed in the US by the *Tasini et al v. The New York Times Co. Inc et al, 2000*, judgement.

A group of journalists had contracted with *The New York Times* for their work to be published in printed form. They never assigned rights for electronic publication. But the *Times* sold the rights of these authors' articles, along with other *Times*' content, to Lexis-Nexis' online database. The court ruled that the paper was not entitled to do this and the journalists won compensation. Precedent from the case will impact on many databases, and similar judgements are likely in other jurisdictions because of the comparability of law.

"The Tasini ruling is a very, very big issue for the online industry, because database providers like Lexis-Nexis have a lot of information that was created – and is therefore still owned – by freelance writers," Keith Kupferschmid, the intellectual property counsel at the US's Software & Information Industry Association, told *Information Today*.

It should be noted, however, that in November 2000 the US Supreme Court announced that it would be reviewing the lower court's decision.

Nevertheless, following the Tasini case a number of other legal actions have been initiated in North America and several outstanding suits have been settled, including cases involving Contentville and UnCover. UnCover, owner of another electronic database of articles, must pay $7.25m to thousands of authors whose work was re-used without permission or payment. The National Writers Union in the US agreed settlements with both UnCover and Contentville, which includes a union payment collection and reimbursement system for authors.

Publishers may now have to choose between paying a proportion of their income to journalists on an ongoing basis, or becoming more assertive in demanding electronic rights from contributors. Either way, the traditional relationships between publishers and contributors have been changed by the web.

According to Bernie Corbett, until recently freelance organiser for the National Union of Journalists in the UK, this 'copyright grab' is largely a feature of Britain and North America where copyright is regarded as a matter of property rights, compared to human rights in European, non-Anglo-Saxon, countries.

By contrast, many academics, long frustrated by the meagre or non-existent fees paid by specialist book publishers and journals, and spiralling journal subscription rates, have chosen to sidetrack publishers. Many now self-publish over the web, and retain copyright ownership, using so-called 'pre-print' and 'e-print' databases.

There have also been legal actions over the downloading and distribution of photos using the web. In one case, *Penthouse.com* took enforcement action against an individual who downloaded 20,000 images from the official web site and made them available free of charge over a newsgroup.

And new threats

The threat the Internet poses to copyright today is of a different magnitude to anything that has gone before. Digital copying, and the ability to generate endless replicas without loss of quality, is not new. What is unique is that the web has made it possible to replicate and distribute multiple copies of copyrighted material to any number of people around the world at the click of a mouse. Additionally, digital copying generally leaves no sign of a copy having been made. For this reason the web has been described by *PC Week* as "the world's biggest copying machine."

A number of recent and current legal actions in the US underline the extent to which copyright infringement is rapidly becoming a serious concern for industries only just coming to terms with the web.

·Music first

The popularity of the MP3 digital format and the growth in use of MP3 players (small pocket-sized audio players that can hold as much as 80 hours of music), have seen a huge increase in music downloaded over the Internet, often bootlegged. MP3 files shrink digital video and audio files by 90% without loss of quality, enabling CDs and DVDs to be easily downloaded from the web.

To support these activities several web services have been established which are in conflict with the music industry. "People who would never walk into a Tower Records and steal a compact disc are doing the same thing on the Internet when they download illegal copies of music," said Tom Silverman, chief executive of Tommy Boy Records, quoted by *E-Commerce Times*.

Lars Ulrich, the drummer of the band Metallica, which brought its own copyright infringement case against the file sharing internet site Napster, told a Congress inquiry: "Napster highjacked our music without asking. Our catalogue of music simply became available as free downloads on the Napster system."

Moreover, the growing internet radio sector will produce further conflicts over copyright ownership. In the US, unlike Europe, copyright payments are made by radio stations only to composers and authors of lyrics, not to performers. Where a radio station broadcasts over the Internet and fails to pay composers and lyricists then ISPs will be required, under the DMCA, to remove access to infringing stations. If a radio station also broadcasts advertising specifically directed at a US audience then US courts are likely to decide they have jurisdiction over the radio station, wherever it is based.

'Pirates' are already testing the boundaries of the fledgling US legislation, and while this growing conflict is primarily being played out in North America, the same issues will soon impact on Europe and Asia.

Industry wins the first round

In April 2000, the music industry won the first round in what looks to be a long, drawn-out struggle. The Recording Industry Association of America (RIAA) convinced a US district judge that the music site MP3.com was infringing the copyright of its members (including all the world's major music companies).

MP3.com had created a database of nearly 80,000 CDs on its servers. Supposedly, these files were for owners of CDs to download their own tracks as MP3 files. The judge did not accept this and ruled that as MP3.com were undertaking the copying on behalf of the consumer this did not come under the provision of 'fair use' for an individual to make personal copies. MP3.com's settlement just with the Warner Music Group and BMG labels cost the company $40m, but with licensing agreements now in place with many of the record labels MP3.com may still have a profitable future.

At the time of publishing there remained confusion over a separate case brought against Napster. Unlike MP3.com, Napster does not store MP3 files itself, merely allowing users to swap their own music files – and Napster has 38 million users doing this. In itself, therefore, Napster does not breach copyright, it provides the means for users to do so.

Moreover, Napster initially claimed that by providing a service on the Internet it was an 'online service provider', under the terms of the DMCA, and therefore given 'safe harbour' from liability for actions of its users. The RIAA applied for, and intitially won, a preliminary injunction to shut the Napster web site down, but Napster then won a stay of execution.

In its defence, Napster later argued – as did MP3.com – that its service is similar to the VCR, and cited the case of Sony which successfully defended its right to manufacture video recorders because people could use them to copy material they had a legal right to copy under 'fair use' regulations.

It remains to be seen whether the announcement in November 2000 of a deal between Napster and Bertelsmann (one of the companies suing Napster) will prove the kiss of death for the file-swapping services, or an acceptance by the music industry that the rules have changed forever.

The implications rippled wider when AOL was persuaded to withdraw its search engine facility for MP3 files, on the grounds that it was unable to distinguish between legal and non-legal MP3 files.

Artists and their managers are reviewing the implications of these cases and considering ways of bypassing record labels through online distribution. The Who now sell tracks over its web site, and Tracy Chapman's manager, Ron Stone, told *Management Today* magazine: "Artists' rights are never discussed in the argument between internet groups and record companies."

More musicians may use the web to market their products, bypassing traditional publishers. In September 2000, the US band The Smashing Pumpkins released tracks over the web free of charge – rapidly distributed through web-based file swapping systems – as a means of punishing its record label Virgin for allegedly not supporting the band sufficiently.

Alan McGee, manager of Oasis, claimed a new approach in his online music publishing business, Poptones, by bringing together online sales of tracks and whole CDs, together with internet radio and TV, underlining the web's opportunities for new business models while threatening old ones.

Although the headline-grabbing legal actions have focused on the music industry, the same potential threat hangs over anyone with copyrighted material in digital form including – as broadband becomes more widely available – the film, radio and television industries. Additionally, any company that stores information in a web-accessible database is potentially at risk as the new generation of file-swapping services can swap any file, whatever format.

Swapping movies

The implications came home to the film industry when it discovered that web site Scour.com was permitting the free trading not just of music but of movies, including some still showing in cinemas. In response, the Motion Picture Association of America (MPAA) immediately applied to the courts to have the service shut down.

And co-founders of Napster, Bill Bales and Adrian Scott, launched AppleSoup using similar programming principles. However, the business case differed, after learning from the law suits against Napster and MP3.com. AppleSoup is financially backed by the former chairman of Universal Studios, Frank Biondi, and intends users to pay to use its network.

When launching the company, Biondi told the press: "AppleSoup has succeeded in finding a way to offer a depth of content to consumers, without violating anyone's rights or intellectual property." He added in advance of releasing details that it was a "copyright-friendly approach." The project is likely to involve copyright owners selling access to their work through a web site, where a film can be downloaded to view at home.

But the film industry is confused as to how to respond to the opportunities and threats posed by the Internet. Studios invested heavily in digitisation of film for internet distribution, in the expectation that films could be released on a pay-per-view basis. This business model was badly damaged by the music industry's experience with MP3.com and Napster, and the wider multimedia file-trading application available at Scour.com. Although Scour.com subsequently filed for bankruptcy, the industry suspended plans for releasing films over the web, and instead are running trailers on their web sites.

A distribution means that the film industry envisaged as providing new revenue streams may just allow consumers to obtain products free of charge, reducing existing income from video sales and rental. While it is important to respond quickly to technological developments, the movie industry failed to have a clear and watertight business model before taking action that threatened existing revenue streams.

The tools for piracy

The threat of the Internet is not solely as a medium for copyright piracy itself. It is also a powerful distribution channel for piracy tools. This was underlined by another legal case in North America, where US journalist Eric Corley was put on trial for spreading, via his online hackers' magazine *2600,* a software utility known as Decode Content Scrambling System (DeCSS) that can disable the encryption system used on DVDs.

The MPAA argued that a technology intended to circumvent systems designed to protect copyrighted material is outlawed by the DMCA. Corley maintained that it was a 'fair use' and free speech issue and was supported by the Electronic Frontier Foundation (EFF), which claimed that without such a utility it would be impossible for users of the Linux operating system to watch DVDs they already own. If the courts outlawed DeCSS, argued the EFF's John Gilmore, it would "become illegal to build open source products that can operate and/or compete with proprietary ones for displaying copyright material." The MPAA won the initial hearing, but the case has gone to appeal.

Web sites distributing copied TV programmes have also faced legal challenge. One of these, iCraveTV, believed it had a defence against copyright actions by agreeing to pay fees to broadcasters – and likened itself to cable stations in Canada that have a public service right to retransmit (without seeking permission) providing they paid into a communal royalties fund. The media industry claimed that broadcasting over the web fundamentally changed the character of the broadcast, not least by producing lower grade reproduction. In December 1999, the MPAA sued, backed by the National Sports League of the US, eight US TV stations and nine Canadian channels.

The MPAA in court called the operation "one of the largest and most brazen thefts of intellectual property ever committed in the United

States." Significantly, action was taken against the Canadian iCraveTV operation under US law because its founder, William Craig, had dual US and Canadian citizenship and US business interests.

The judge agreed with the television companies and granted a temporary restraining order, blocking iCraveTV from transmitting the copyrighted programmes into the US "via the iCraveTV.com site or any other internet sites or any online facility of any kind."

The web site agreed to arbitration with the TV stations, and the outcome was that iCraveTV ceased broadcasting over the web until a legal precedent became established. The action failed to resolve underlying legal issues, especially where they do not involve a US national, and with hundreds of thousands of users attracted to the first TV programme recording web sites, the business model of pay-tv over the web seems viable. The questions are who controls the process, and how and what fees will eventually be charged.

The web fights back

Success by the RIAA against MP3.com and Napster, and by MPAA against iCraveTV, may be irrelevant in the longer term. A new generation of 'peer-to-peer' (P2P) services is proliferating on the web, providing a much greater threat to copyright holders.

One such service, Gnutella, was written by AOL employees. Appalled by the legal implications of its distribution, and AOL's potential liability, company executives withdrew it permanently within hours of it going up on AOL's system. But a few hours is a long time on the Internet, and once out Gnutella stayed out. Since then it has been widely distributed and improved on by an army of open source software programmers.

Another software utility, Freenet, was designed by British programmer Ian Clarke. Unlike Napster, new generation services like Freenet are entirely distributed, and have no central server. There is generally no company responsible. Outraged copyright owners have no one to sue and no service to shut down.

That these services are a direct threat to IP cannot be doubted. When asked to comment on the potential of Freenet to allow copyright theft, Ian Clarke commented to online news service, *etown.com*: "Stealing implies that you're dealing with property. I disagree with people who say information is the same as other forms of property. I'm not so sure you can treat information like real estate or gold."

ISP liability

ISPs have been targeted by those trying to protect their copyright who hope that ISPs might act as the Internet's gatekeeper. So, should ISPs establish monitoring devices and defensive walls to prevent subscribers copying items that are copyrighted?

In Germany, a court ruled that AOL Germany broke copyright law by failing to take action to prevent subscribers swapping pirated music. But in another case, involving the AOL subsidiary CompuServe in Germany, an originally successful prosecution of its director, for allegedly enabling child pornography to be viewed by not blocking subscribers' access to web sites containing it, was overturned on appeal and the director acquitted. It was recognised that the director could not have foreseen the child pornography use; nor could the company have technically blocked users' access.

But the Church of Scientology has successfully taken a series of legal actions in both the US and Europe against ISPs obliging them to remove copyright-infringing material from web sites they host.

Concerns that ISPs do not have the same protection from liability in Europe as in the US were fuelled by the *Demon v Godfrey* case, in which Dr Laurence Godfrey sued Demon Internet for a libel against him on a Demon-hosted newsgroup. The key factor, which told against Demon, was that it failed to remove libellous material after Dr Godfrey advised the company of it. As we will see below, the requirement on ISPs to remove infringing material when notified has subsequently been written into the EU's Electronic Commerce Directive, and it remains the case that ISPs are not protected from defamation or copyright breaches if they fail to remove infringing content once it has been brought to their attention.

Legal inconsistencies in different jurisdictions complicate the question of ISP liability for copyright infringement. To encourage harmonisation on ISP liability, WIPO set out guidance to governments in 1999. "Because the Internet is a borderless medium and its markets are global, it is critical that compatible approaches to this issue [of ISP liability for subscribers' breach of copyright] be adopted around the world," it said. "It is not necessary that the approaches be identical; they may differ depending on the particular circumstances and legal traditions in any given country. But they must be interoperable if global networks and electronic commerce are to develop smoothly."

It added that the 1996 WIPO Copyright Treaty determined that merely providing the wires of communication does not constitute communication, but that this does not necessarily cover the situation of ISPs.

In the wake of this WIPO treaty, the 1998 DMCA radically updated copyright law in the US. The DMCA specifically provided exemptions to ISPs, not holding them responsible for copyright breaches undertaken by their subscribers.

The EU's 2000 Electronic Commerce Directive was closely modelled on the DMCA, and copyright protection is similar. However, the e-commerce directive covers wider matters of ISP liability (such as defamation), whereas the DMCA, as the name implies, only covers copyright.

Under the European e-commerce directive, ISPs and telecommunications operators are not liable for information transmitted if they neither initiate transmission, nor select receivers of transmissions. Intermediaries are also exempt from prosecution where they are found to be storing infringing content, provided they have no knowledge of its illegal nature. Thus there is no duty on intermediaries to monitor information they store or transmit. But a 'notice and take down' procedure must operate, whereby they remove infringing material brought to their attention.

The directive does, however, allow some minor points to be resolved at a national level, such as details of who is allowed to freely copy copyrighted material under 'fair use' provisions. There are also some other technical differences between the EU and US laws[1]. The key differences concerning copyright, between the two sets of legislation, are the level of regulation on the 'notice and take down' procedures. These are quite tightly defined in the US, but are more a matter of self-regulation in the EU with member states left to decide on any detailed regulation they wish to impose.

But there is concern, not least from the US Government, that the carefully crafted provisions of the Electronic Commerce Directive, which defines protection for ISPs, may be undone by the proposed Copyright Directive. Lawyers believe that, in its draft form, the Copyright Directive's broad-brush approach to immunity from liability could remove the 'notice and take down' requirements.

Internet portals, such as auction sites and retail malls, that are not themselves selling goods but acting as gateways to shops and individuals selling goods also face legal uncertainty. It appears that these may have a duty to comply with national laws following the outcome of a case in France against Yahoo. This barred access, via the French Yahoo web site only, to Nazi memorabilia sold through Yahoo's auction site. Yet French nationals were still able to access the same material via Yahoo's US, and other, sites. The same legal principles could affect copyright cases.

Moreover, there is a wider range of products that can breach copyright than is commonly realised. The manufacture of counterfeit textile goods can be a breach of copyright, and the unauthorised reproduction of a cartoon character could also be a copyright infringement. Indeed, the growth of the Internet has indirectly led to a spate of burglaries in London fashion houses where thieves have stolen the latest fashion designs, digitised the drawings and emailed them to the Far East where cheap and illegally produced fashionwear can be produced just days after a design has first appeared on the catwalk. And, bizarrely, online

---

[1] *See Online Provider Liability for Copyright Infringement by Kamiel Koelman and Professor Bernt Hugenholtz, www.wipo.int/eng/meetings/1999/osp/pdf/osp_lia1.pdf*

data swapping has included middle-aged mothers sharing needlework patterns to avoid buying them.

Copyright theft has entered new territories through web technology and speed.

Hyperlinks at issue

It is becoming clear, as more case history is established, that hyperlinks, too, may breach copyright. The most famous dispute saw the MPAA sue the online hacker magazine *2600* for linking to DeCSS software that decrypts DVDs. The MPAA attempted to close down hyperlinks from *2600* to web sites containing the DeCSS program, arguing that since one site performs an illegal function it must be illegal to link to it. The magazine eventually sidestepped the issue by replacing the hyperlink with the domain address. The same principles underlined the legal action against Napster – it did nothing illegal, but enabled others to do so.

The US courts have ruled in the case *Ticketmaster v. Tickets.com* that it is not illegal for one site to link to another, even where permission has not been granted. The judge said: "Hyperlinking does not in itself involve a violation of the Copyright Act." And the DMCA makes clear that ISPs linking to infringing material are not liable for copyright infringement. Yet it fails to clarify whether linking itself is an infringement. Most lawyers appear to believe that hyperlinks are not a copyright breach, but some take the opposite view, and there is a lack of clear legal precedent within any jurisdiction.

In the UK the situation is particularly unclear because of a dispute between *The Shetland News* and *The Shetland Times*, which went to court. The *News* created a link deep into the web content of the *Times*, without the latter's permission. The *Times* sued the *News* for breach of copyright, but only an interim interdict – in favour of the *Times*, recognising it had a prima facie case – under Scottish law was granted. Rather than complete the court action, the parties agreed that the link could stay in place provided that the *News* placed the *Times* logo next to each linked headline.

One interpretation of the situation, in many jurisdictions, is that hyperlinks that go direct to an article on another web site may be a breach of copyright because they bypass advertising on the home page which subsidises content.

Databases

Databases, many of which are now accessible over the Internet, can also be protected by copyright. The legal principles laid down in the US – in *Feist Publications Ltd v. Rural Telephone Service Co Inc 1991* – are that, firstly, copyright protection exists to increase the total wealth of knowledge in society, not to reward publishers or authors, and, secondly, that facts and ideas cannot be copyrighted. A telephone directory cannot be copyrighted because, while compilers have exercised effort in obtaining information, the work produced is not an original work of authorship.

Similar principles were established in the EU by the 1991 case, *Van Dale v. Romme*, heard by the Supreme Court of the Netherlands, where it was held that a database is only protected by copyright if it reflects the 'personal vision' of its originator. Although databases – including the many that are, or will be, stored over the web – are in principle copyrightable, many will fail the tests of originality and authorship.

An early EU step towards digital copyright law was its 1996 Directive for the Legal Protection of Databases, which recognised that databases could be protected by copyright where they were works of sufficient originality. However, as Professor Bernt Hugenholtz of the Institute for Information Law at the University of Amsterdam says: "Complete libraries have been devoted to the concept of originality. 'Clear definitions' [on this] do not exist in copyright law. The US Feist case contains extensive discussion of the concept of originality in US copyright law. The originality requirement under the EU Database Directive is defined as 'the author's own intellectual creation'." What this means in practice is for the courts to resolve.

The EU Database Directive provides further protection of a 'sui generis' (of its own kind) right. This provides specific and additional protection to databases where there has been 'substantial investment'. Trevor Cook, a database specialist at the UK law firm Bird & Bird, says that here, too, the actual definition is unclear and courts must resolve matters on a case by case basis. Moreover, the 'sui generis' protection does not apply to all databases used within the EU. "Such protection is only available to European database makers and to those based in other countries which give similar protection to European databases, i.e. not the USA," points out Mr Cook.

WIPO is now considering proposals for this 'sui generis' right to be exported across the rest of the world, where it is not currently recognised. However, the US Government believes that the EU Database Directive "is overly restrictive" and opposes a comparable 'sui generis' right applying in the US. But bills have been proposed in the US House of Representatives – but not, as yet, passed – to provide greater protection against 'misappropriation' of databases, without going as far as the EU's 'sui generis' rights.

Recent case law, particularly in the US, is helping to define the extent to which databases are covered by copyright, and alternative means by which database owners can protect their investments. One of the most important cases so far heard was *Jurisline v. Reed Elsevier*. Jurisline purchased a CD-Rom published by Lexis-Nexis, a division of Reed Elsevier, that contained information compiled by the US Government which Jurisline claimed was therefore public domain content not protected by copyright. But Jurisline's representative, in making the purchase, consented to a licensing agreement which accepted that information contained on the CD-Rom would not be reproduced, although Jurisline intended to use the content for its own web-based research service for the legal profession.

Legal action was initiated by Jurisline against Reed Elsevier, claiming that Lexis-Nexis was seeking legal protection where none was justified, inflating the cost of its product which was reproduced public domain information and involved in a monopoly supply arrangement of legal information. Jurisline settled the case, and the associated counter-suit from Reed, because the court ruled that the license agreement from Lexis-Nexis was valid and enforceable, even though it was protecting non-copyrightable content. Jurisline was therefore forced to withdraw all content from its web site that originated from the Lexis-Nexis CD-Rom.

This case highlights the possibility that copyright may play a decreasingly important role in the web environment. More publishers may choose to protect their original work, not by resorting to copyright law that may be impossible to enforce over the web, but through contracts supported by licensing agreements, which may be enforceable (see chapter six).

Where now?

Cases like Napster and DeCSS have led some in the US to suggest that the DMCA is already out of date. However, drawing attention to the difficulties that the law faces in keeping up with technology may encourage those who believe that traditional IP acts as a brake on internet development.

When members of the US Senate Judiciary Committee met to examine the issues raised by the proliferation of music swapping services, it emerged that fans of Napster and MP3.com had deluged two US senators with 70,000 email messages. With votes at stake such actions could encourage politicians to rethink the role of IP law. Senators noted, reported *PC World*, "that laws designed to protect intellectual property could crush technological innovation."

We can expect to see new approaches developed for detecting infringement. Several universities use artificial intelligence systems to compare student essays against material published on the web to check whether students have committed plagiarism. Similar methods could prove useful in detecting copyright infringement. There are also a growing number of digital rights management systems (DRMs) being developed to deter infringement (see chapter five).

However, as WIPO points out: "No matter how ingenious the technology used to protect works against unauthorised use, equally ingenious ways may be developed to circumvent it."

Owners of copyright have to accept that it may simply not be possible to protect content on the Internet. Commenting on the new P2P services, Freenet's Ian Clarke advises businesses to accept that copyright protection is simply no longer possible. "I have two words for these companies: 'give up'," he told the *New York Times*. "There is no way they are going to stop these technologies. They are trying to plug holes in a dam that is about to burst." Clarke added, when talking to *The Independent*: "Freenet destabalises the record companies' business model as it's set-up at present. But whether the business model they presently use is the best one for the future is a different question."

One thing is clear: copyright owners cannot just ignore the challenges offered by the Internet and hope they have little impact. These are interesting times for copyright owners and they need to act quickly – or they may find that the web has simply put them out of business.

Paul Gosling interviews Andrew Yeates, Director General of the British Phonographic Industry

Q: Do you believe that 'the web changes everything' when it comes to copyright ownership?

A: *No, I don't. It's an evolutionary process. If you look back over the years, copyright has developed to respond to new technologies: for example, accommodating the introduction of sound recordings and broadcasting. Online delivery covers some rights that are now well established and some new rights recognised by international initiatives such as the 1996 WIPO Treaties.*

Q: How important do you believe the web-based file sharing systems such as Napster, MP3.com, Gnutella and Freenet are? To what extent do they change the realities of copyright on the web?

A: *The principle about intellectual property is that creativity deserves a reward. Computer software is a creative work. Exploitation of these creative works should generate opportunity for reward. The reality is that many file-sharing systems provide opportunities, which should be embraced. But if the only purpose of a new development is to deprive existing copyright owners of their work, then infringing or inciting infringement of copyright is not legitimate. If it is done in the spirit of legitimate co-operation then it should be viewed positively.*

Q: Do you think the issues over copyright are roughly the same, or mainly different, when looking at content, music, software, film etc.?

A: *Copyright protection has evolved to protect unauthorised use of owners' 'property'. Uses are recognised and added to with advances in technology. The right to copy a work has been joined by a right to broadcast a work. The rights apply generally across all genres of works. In the online environment it will be important to look at each type of copyright work and define the 'uses' that are involved in the work being made available, deliv-*

ered and accessed by consumers. So yes, broadly the issues are the same.

Q: Is there not a real problem in stopping copyright infringement on the web, given that the IP is already 'out there' in unprotected digital format – CDs. How can millions of CD owners be stopped from swapping music with the peer-to-peer systems available on the Internet?

A: *Of course it is a problem. But piracy has been a problem for creative industries since the beginning. The biggest problem is the lack of protection. If you look at the UK then piracy in the 'traditional markets' is reasonably well controlled. In many other countries piracy accounts for 70%, or more, of sales. What pressure does that put on people who operate legitimately in a country which does not recognise IP at the level recognised within the United Kingdom?*

The answer is to ask governments to work together and harmonise protection in each territory. The recorded music industry is particularly concerned about cross-European implementation of provisions in the European Union's draft Copyright Directive relevant to delivery of material online. If the framework does not allow copyright owners to develop technologies to enforce copyright protection when material is delivered online, then we will not stay one step ahead of the hackers.

Q: Aren't the copyright owners just defending their own interests? How can musicians' and consumers' interests be best advanced?

A: *Musicians are performers. Performers deserve recognition for their work.*

Record companies represent musicians. A lot of the arguments that the music business acts against the interests of consumers by restricting distribution is misconstrued, in that any content can be used by these software packages and this can damage anyone whose works are reproduced without consent. We are doing nothing different from other content owners. There is self-interest. But like anyone else, who manufactures goods, you need a return to carry on running a successful business.

Q: Is the music industry scared that the web will provide opportunities for copyright generators – the musicians – to bypass the traditional owners of copyright by going direct to their audience? How should record labels and other traditional copyright owners respond to this threat?

A: *This is a bit of a myth. If an artist decides not to use a record company, but to record their own music to release on the Internet, the copyright system means that the person who makes the sound recording owns the sound recording. When a record company makes an investment in artists it is spent in A&R, marketing, profile-building, and branding to enable the music to sell. In terms of copyright that investment is the issue. If you do that, and you own the sound recording, it is reasonable that you have the ability to earn a reward. That applies whether you are a record label or a musician.*

Q: What business models do you believe will emerge as the most successful as the means of exploiting copyright in the web environment?

A: *In the longer term there will be increased streaming of on-demand material to consumers. But for people to know which they want there will have to be guides and consumer aides, such as electronic programme guides. These will help people find content they want and need, and also to find what they don't know they want, but which stimulates an interest. The danger is that by supplying three million streams of information to someone who has never used a PC, consumers will reject the service because they do not know 'where to start'.*

Q: Do you think that new legislation, such as the DMCA, is helping or hindering the process of adapting copyright to the web?

A: *The DMCA is helpful, particularly in the States, because it has brought a higher level of protection for sound recordings. But until you get a completely harmonised system around the world different interpretations will cause difficulties for global broadcasting, such as on the web. For example, webcasting means different things in different territories around the world.*

Q: Are you concerned that the US is creating the world's ground rules for copyright protection, driven by a desire to look after the country's major corporations? If so, how do believe Europe and Asia should respond to the US leadership?

A: *The reality must be that evolution of copyright legislation is global – you must look at all countries in the world. It is natural that there are territories that rely on IP protection because their economies currently generate income from these rights. Others have very high piracy rates. The emphasis will be different. Therefore, the fact that the US is pressing some key issues to protect IP has to be a good thing. The fact they might not currently fully provide for some rights recognised outside the US is an ongoing concern – for example, the right for owners of sound recordings to obtain remuneration for the traditional broadcasting of their works – and is something we should focus on and ask for harmonisation upwards to the UK level.*

Q: Can you foresee an alternative to copyright that is better suited to the web and which protects IP rights?

A: *No. Copyright should be absolutely key to the framework. What we may need to do is define and refine rights relevant to delivery online. This might cover the public's rights of 'access' to computer software programs that make available downloads in return for a fee or subscription. This would reflect new business models applying these new rights. At the same time, traditional uses involved in the new business models should not be forgotten. Copying can be copying in copyright terms, regardless of the technology used!*

Q: What do you believe that other areas of copyright – video, broadcasting, movies – can and should learn from the experience of the music industry in its copyright protection legal actions?

A: *The new software packages being developed will affect all content owners. Content on DVDs is already affected. It will not be long before all forms of content face similar problems. The music industry has faced these issues first because it is a technology-friendly industry and it attracts young people willing to experiment. But that should not be an argument to take away protection.*

Q: Is the BPI involved in any initiatives to develop new digital rights management tools or standards to protect copyright on the web? Can these provide a solution?

A: *Yes. We are involved in wider industry projects. We are looking at what is being developed. We are the UK national group of International Federation of the Phonographic Industry (IFPI). IFPI is involved in a number of content industry initiatives such as Secure Digital Music Initiative (SDMI). The BPI operates an Anti-Piracy Unit, which is constantly monitoring new developments and assessing whether these are being made available in ways which provide opportunities or threats to the legitimate use of BPI members' repertoire.*

Q: Can a technological defence system for copyright work?

A: *You have to look at the way each defence system would work in practice. Will it be accepted and/or used by the ultimate consumer? Different systems will have different levels of effectiveness depending on the services/delivery systems to which they are applied. Digital terrestrial television transmissions intended for reception by the public at basic subscription rates will not need to be encrypted at the same level as a highly prized programme only available to selected subscribers on demand.*

Investment in appropriate technical protection measures should be properly recognised by governments. In the latest text of the draft EC Copyright Directive there is recognition of the need for content industries such as the record industry to use technology to protect and deliver works to the consumer. If a government believes that the technology does not provide for 'enough copying' to cover copyright exceptions, it leaves the possibility for EU governments to intervene in an ad hoc manner with technology developed to provide new choices of delivery to the consumer.

Government interference is not the way forward. Such interference would create uncertainty for content, computer and electronic industries over what copy protection would be acceptable. This in turn would adversely affect investment and development of new technology/encryption systems, which could benefit consumers.

Paul Gosling interviews Richard Stallman, founder of the GNU Project, which developed the GNU free operating system

Q: Do you believe that the web changes everything when it comes to copyright ownership?

A: *The web in particular, no – but computers and computer networks make a tremendous difference in how we have to evaluate, ethically, systems of copyright. The system of copyright was intended to benefit the public. The public traded away certain freedoms that it couldn't really exercise, and in exchange got the benefit of more books being written and published.*

The freedom that the public traded away, which the public couldn't exercise effectively, was the freedom to make copies of books, which in the age of the printing press could only feasibly be done by setting the type and printing a run of copies. In other words only by publishing. So, in effect, copyright was a restriction only on publishers and on authors. It was an industrial regulation, and that is what made copyright useful, acceptable, easy to enforce and painless.

But digital information technology makes it easier for people to copy and manipulate information and it has made it possible for the general public to exercise the freedom to copy works. It is now a useful freedom for us all to have and as a result we can no longer afford to trade it away. It is no longer a good deal for the public – at least not in its present form. So we have to reconsider the deal. Some of this freedom to copy works we should keep and use, rather than trading it away.

Q: Do you think that the issues over copyright are roughly the same or mainly different when looking at content, music, software, film, etc?

A: *I dislike the word 'content' because it makes things sound like a commodity, and I don't want to treat them as a commodity, so I am not going to use that word. The issues are not entirely the same for different kinds of works. I think that the issues vary according to how the works are used. Some kinds of works are functional – that is, they are used to get a job done – such as computer programs, recipes, manuals, text books and anything used to study something, that teaches you how to do something, and reference books. For all those functional works I believe the issues are essentially the same. People should have the freedom not only to redistribute those, but even to publish modified versions. If something is used to get a job done, well your job may not be the same as somebody else's job, so the work that is good for him may not be right for you, and you should be able to adapt it to serve your needs and publish that because there may be other people who have needs like yours.*

But there are other kinds of works, which represent somebody's views, or experience, or thoughts; these include memoirs, offers to buy and sell, scientific papers, and essays which argue for positions. I think it is not a good idea to modify those because that's falsifying the views of the person they represent. But redistributing verbatim should be permitted, more or less. For example, everybody should be free to redistribute a scientific paper.

There is another class of works, which are mainly for aesthetic purposes – works that are artistic. And for them I am not sure what I think about making modified versions. There are arguments on both sides.

Q: Will the legal cases against Napster, 2600 and MP3.com resolve anything?

A: *That question seems to be based on the idea that what we need is a resolution – that any answer is o.k., as long as it is an answer. I don't believe that. We don't need to 'resolve' something, we need to win back our freedoms. Those legal cases will affect the development of the area, but whether they will win us back our*

*freedom remains to be seen. I would suspect that the people will
have the last word no matter what the courts do.*

Q: To what extent should copyright still be used as a means of
distributing revenues to people who authored work?

A: *Having copyright covering commercial distribution would be a
way of doing that. I am not saying that copyright has to be
entirely abolished for all kinds of work, not even on the Internet.*

Q: Isn't there a risk that writers and musicians, and software
writers, end up not being properly paid?

A: *Well most of them are not properly paid now. I think that criti-
cising the alternative is the pot calling the kettle black. I read
recently that musicians get 4% of CD revenue. The famous
musicians have the clout to get much more than that, which
shows that many musicians get much less than that. So it is a
very bad system. I believe we can find other systems that work
just as well, which don't involve restrictions on people's rights.*

Q: But don't some of the copyright owners at least deserve a return
on their investment?

A: *Not at the cost of denying us our freedom.*

Q: Isn't there a risk that if publishers lose their reward they won't
be commissioning writers?

A: *There is no need for publishers if people are distributing their
works over the Internet. To the extent that people are still getting
printed copies of course they still need publishers. But with the
Internet, why can't a writer be his own publisher?*

Q.: Are you worried by the role of the US in creating the world's
ground rules for copyright law?

A: *It is the wrong country to take a lead because it is in the pocket
of the media companies. The US government doesn't even
consider the needs of its own public and it considers the interests
of the public of other countries even less.*

Q: And how should European and Asian governments respond to this?

A: *They should consider what is best for their countries.*

Q: You have said that the US is adopting Soviet-style techniques to enforce the rules on copyright ownership.

A: *I use this expression not just to express my disapproval of it. The actual methods used are parallel, except in small details, to those used in the Soviet Union to stamp out unauthorised copying. Because the government didn't like it, it used authoritarian measures against it. Guards on all copying equipment to watch what is being copied; harsh punishments for people engaged in unauthorised copying; to seek informers to rat on their co-workers; and collective responsibility, conscripting people for surveillance on other people and punishing the one if any of the others is caught doing forbidden copying. And propaganda stating that only a vicious enemy of the people would do this illegal copying. In the US the propaganda word 'pirate' is used if you share data with your neighbour.*

Q: Where does 'free software' fit into the debate on copyright on the web?

A: *Free software is software that everybody is free to copy or modify. It becomes free software because the author has authorised copying or modification. Free software is an example of developing material without obstructing its use and its users.*

Q: If the example of free software and non-copyright material on the web is accepted then new business models are needed. Can you think of business models that you believe will fit the web?

A: *For software there seem to be a number of models that work. The best people to ask about that are the 'open source' people who have taken the ideas of free software and discarded the ethical considerations that are the foundation for us and focused on practical benefits alone. Selling copies of free software and manuals are possible. Remember that the 'free' in free software refers to freedom not price, so it is possible to sell copies of free software and there are many companies selling free software. Making money from software development is not, in itself, wrong. And you can be paid to write a specific program that a client needs.*

Q: You've pioneered the 'copyleft' technique. Can you briefly explain the principles behind copyleft?

A: *It's a technique we use to make sure that a program remains free for all users. We use the existing copyright system but in the opposite way it is normally used: so we use copyright to get copyleft. We say this program is copyrighted, which means that legally by default it is not allowed to be copied or modified. But then we say you are authorised to copy this software; you are authorised to modify this software; you are authorised to distribute modified versions. But there are conditions, that whenever you redistribute anything that is in whole or part based on this software, under these conditions anyone who gets it from you gets these same freedoms about copying and modifying. In this way the freedom goes wherever the software goes. Whoever gets the software gets the freedom.*

Q: If governments and corporations refuse to accept this vision, do you believe that there is a technological defence system out there that could work to protect copyright?

A: *I object to the word 'protect'. It's a propaganda word. I don't believe that copyright protects a program or a song, because I don't believe that a program is 'damaged' by being run by more people, or a song is 'damaged' by being played by more people.*

As for your question, no. All such systems can be bypassed and therefore they depend on draconian laws prohibiting people bypassing them.

Chapter Three
Trademarks and domain names: uncomfortable bedfellows
By Hugh Brett

Trademarks

Trademarks have a long history. They are a form of shorthand that indicates the source of goods by words or logos. A trademark says that a product has a particular origin. When we buy a Britvic orange drink we expect it to come from Britvic, and a Rolls Royce engine should be manufactured by Rolls Royce.

But trademarks have come under stress from the use of proprietary domain names on the Internet where names, which are either identical or similar to known trademarks, have been registered by others. The question is what can trademark owners do about those who use their names either globally, or in a single legal jurisdiction?

The use of trademarks can be traced to the very early days of commerce when Roman potters placed their marks on pieces of pottery to identify and indicate their source, or when cattle were branded with a sign to indicate ownership. Hence the term 'brands' – a name often used to denote valuable trademarks.

For many years trademarks were unregulated because there was no formal system of regulation, or office where trademarks could be registered. The industrial revolution and the growth of consumer demand for manufactured products created the need for a system whereby products could be identified formally with particular manufacturers.

The demand for product identification was met by the establishment of a Trademark Office in 1875 in the UK, and has been followed by other national trademark offices throughout the world. The purpose of a trademark office is to examine and record the registration of trademarks. In 1998, a Community Trademark Office was set up in Alicante, Spain, to handle European Community (now European Union) trademarks.

Trademark offices are not merely recorders of trademark applications – they examine applications to ensure that they meet formal requirements. Trademark offices employ professional trademark examiners who consider trademark applications to ensure that each trademark application is genuine and distinctive. Each application has to be made within a defined class of goods or services, such as books, beverages, software or food.

Applications, which are not distinctive or are too descriptive, will be rejected. A trademark application to register 'soap' as a trademark for cosmetic products would be rejected as too descriptive, as would an application for a geographical name like 'France'. Procedures allow applicants to argue in support of their applications and for others to oppose registration. A registered trademark's validity may be challenged not only before but also after it has been registered. Trademarks continue forever if they are renewed every 10 years and the trademark office's fees are paid. As such, they are a form of property and can be sold and licensed.

Trademark features

An application for a trademark must be made in respect of a specified class of goods or services, but it cannot relate to all goods and/or services. A trademark registration applies only to the country in which it is registered. A trademark registered in Germany or Argentina, say, for 'woolworths' will only apply and be effective in Germany and Argentina. Trademark registrations are therefore territorial in scope. They may be owned by unconnected companies in different countries.

Not all trademarks are registered. The term 'trademarks' is widely used to include unregistered marks. In the absence of registration, the owner of an unregistered trademark has the burden of proving title to it in order to succeed in an infringement action. International marketing practice generally means that registered trademarks are identified by the sign ® and unregistered trademarks with the initials TM.

Domain names

Trademarks were developed to assist businesses to identify their goods/services in the marketplace. The birth of the domain name system, in contrast, was created for reasons unconnected with business needs.

Domain names arose as a result of a technical requirement – a computer needs a number to communicate on the Internet. Domain names reflect a unique number, which is recognised by computers throughout the world. The domain name acts as shorthand to identify an internet address, and it often has the added advantage of being easily remembered.

National domain name registries issue country code domain names. Most registries are independent of government having been created through private initiatives in the scientific community. Domain names issued out of national registries are identified by a country code. Country code top-level domains (ccTLDs) for the United Kingdom are .uk and .fr is for France.

The domain name system also includes three major top-level domain names – .com, .org and .net – which do not have a country code. These are administered by Network Solutions Inc. (NSI), a US registry which is now under the control of the Internet Corporation for Assigned

Names and Numbers (ICANN). ICANN is a non-profit company formed with the encouragement of the US government to manage top-level domain names reflecting global needs. These generic top-level domains (gTLDs) represent about a third of all the 10 million domain names registered. Non-US nationals own many gTLDs. As we will see, major disputes over the control over the use of domain names have been directed towards the control and ownership of the gTDLs – .com, .org and .net.

National domain name registries have developed organically from within the scientific community, which has made its own rules and fee structure. Nominet UK, the UK registry, will not accept domain names with two letters or less. Some registries require the applicant to be a national and others limit the number of domain names per person.

If the domain name system is compared with the trademark system, it can be seen that the domain name system differs significantly from trademark registration. Domain name registries have no extensive examination procedures and if the domain name is free then it is 'first-come, first-registered'. No search is undertaken to establish whether there is any conflict with trademarks or earlier names.

There is no requirement that the name should be distinctive to the applicant. If the domain name 'Cartier' is available it will be registered in the name of the first applicant. Descriptive domain names are registrable – such as www.furniture.co.uk. So, too, are individuals' own names. So, bertieahern.com and bertieahernsucks.com were registered by an entrepreneur of a different name, unconnected to the Irish Prime Minister Bertie Ahern.

Domain names are not territorial – they belong to cyberspace and can be accessed anywhere in the world. The renewal period for domain names is two years, which is much shorter than for trademarks. The cost of registering a domain name – about £80 – is minimal compared to trademark applications, which cost hundreds of pounds.

Domain names v. trademarks

Domain names conflict with trademarks when similar names have different owners. Both identities have commercial value, creating a cyberspace collision. A domain name on the Internet is a powerful indication of origin and trademark/brand owners, such as McDonalds, have been angered to see their trademarks appear as domain names and registered by unconnected businesses without their authority.

Brand owners have been particularly upset by entrepreneurs registering their trademarks with the intention of selling the domain names back to them. This practice is called 'cyber-squatting'. The 'early bird' squatter may, alternatively, register a confusingly similar domain name to a trademark for consumers who misspell a well-known domain name to enter another web site by accident – this is called 'typo-squatting'.

The loss of valuable domain names to cyber-squatters has provoked brand owners to lobby for a series of legal initiatives to prevent the highjacking of brands and to create procedures for the recovery of acknowledged names.

Cyber-squatting in the US

US trademark owners faced significant difficulties when seeking to recover domain names from cyber-squatters. They had to prove that the domain name would lead to commercial confusion and, in some cases, it was not possible to satisfy a judge that a mere domain registration was likely to create public confusion in the marketplace and therefore constituted an infringement of a trademark.

In exceptional cases, where the name that was 'coined' was well-known and the defendant's behaviour was considered by the US court to be disreputable, the judges were prepared to intervene. One example concerned www.panavision.com, which was owned by a cyber-squatter. This cyber-squatter had registered other domain names including aircanda.com, and yankeestadium.com and the court believed this would "eliminate the capacity of the Panavision marks to identify and distinguish Panavision's goods and services on the Internet." The court ordered the transfer of the domain name to Panavision Inc.

But the rate of loss of domain names to cyber-squatters was such that trademark owners set out to lobby for a change in the law. They successfully persuaded the US government, which agreed to amend the US Trademark Act – The Lanham Act – by introducing the Anti-Cybersquatting Consumer Protection Act in November 1999.

The benefits of the Anti-Cybersquatting Act gives registered and unregistered trademark owners, and personalities with well-known names, the right to reclaim confusingly similar domain names if the domain name was registered in 'bad faith'. Factors indicative of 'bad faith' include offers to sell the domain name and the acquisition of multiple domain names. The US Act not only makes straight forward cyber-squatting unlawful, but also typo-squatting since the definition of 'bad faith' includes an intention to divert and mislead customers from a legitimate site.

Damages of up to $100,000 per domain name may be claimed. In addition, the Act introduces a novel procedure to overcome difficulties associated with initiating legal actions against difficult-to-find owners of domain names, including those who live outside the US. A legal action to reclaim a domain name may begin without serving proceedings on the 'moveable' address of a domain name owner. The action may be initiated by bringing the action 'in rem' against the domain name itself, without involving the owner.

Trademark owners in the US now have a powerful means to defend themselves from domain name cyber-squatting. Following the legal reforms, cyber-squatters can be quickly and easily challenged in court.

Cyber-squatting in the UK

UK courts have adapted traditional legal remedies to permit owners of well-known names to recover 'lost' domain names. The legality of the practice of warehousing domain names and selling them on was reviewed in the English courts in the autumn of 1998.

One in a Million Ltd collected and registered well-known business names as domain names, including www.ladbroke.com, www.sainsbury.com and www.marksandspencer.com. The company offered to sell the domain names to the brand owners, but they refused to be blackmailed into buying domain names, which they considered to be their property. They sought legal remedy, arguing that their trademarks had been infringed.

The action was not as simple as might first appear, because to succeed in a trademark infringement action it is necessary to show a competing 'commercial activity' which may lead to consumer confusion. It was argued by One in a Million Ltd that all it had done was to register domain names, there was nothing unlawful in this and no one had been confused.

But the Court of Appeal disagreed. It said that if the domain name www.marksandspencer.com was made the subject of an online search, the likelihood was that any member of the public searching the register would assume that the domain name revealed was connected to the famous store. It concluded, therefore, that the registrations were potential 'instruments of deception' and ordered the domain names to be transferred to the trademark owners.

The judge was clearly influenced by the financial motives of the domain name owners in registering the domain names. One of the letters from the company said, in effect, "Further to our telephone conversation earlier this evening. I confirm that I own the domain name burgerking.co.uk. I would be willing to sell the domain name for the sum of £25,000."

Not all owners of UK trademarks have been successful in using their trademark rights to reclaim domain names. If the domain name registration is innocently made the courts are unlikely to order the domain name to be transferred, as when the large US sports company Prince

Inc. failed to reclaim the domain name www.prince.co.uk from a small UK consultancy firm trading under the name 'Prince'.

Cyber-squatting elsewhere

In other countries, particularly those with civil law backgrounds, the courts have not been restrained by the need to show commercial activity. They have applied general principles of unfair business practices to control cyber-squatting.

The champagne houses have been successful in obtaining the order of a French court for the removal of the domain name www.champagnecereales.com, and the French perfume manufacturer, Guy Laroche, obtained an order of the court for the return of domain name www.guylaroche.com. The French tennis star, Amelie Mauresmo, won a battle off the tennis court by reclaiming the domain name www.mauresmo.com. In Italy, Compaq SpA retrieved the domain name altavista.it, registered by a Mr Bazzacco, on the grounds of trademark infringement and unfair competition.

Ikea, the furniture chainstore, won the first cyber-squatting case in China over ownership of the domain name www.ikea.cn. The Beijing court rejected the implausible explanation that 'ikea' had been created out of a combination of the letter 'i', standing for internet, and the word 'kea', the name of a New Zealand parrot.

The courts worldwide have been willing to extend traditional legal principles to control the practice of mercenary cyber-squatting of well-known names, but not all trademark owners' complaints will succeed. In the case of a unique and individually coined name, the court may infer that the domain name may have been abusively registered. But where the domain name is reasonably commonplace or has been registered perfectly innocently, the trademark owner may fail to reclaim the domain name. This was illustrated by the failure of McDonalds, the burger chain, to obtain the Maltese domain name 'McDonalds' which a café owner with that name had registered for himself at the Maltese domain name registry.

The role of domain name registries

National domain name registries might be expected to control the abusive registration of domain names. However, they are generally reluctant to take on similar roles to those of a trademark office by examining domain name applications. They prefer to follow 'the first-to-file, first-registered' principle. The practices of domain name registries differ in some ways, with each country adopting its own procedural rules restricting the number of domain name applications that may be made by one person or company, and the nationality of applicants.

The rules of the UK domain name registry, Nominet UK, reserves the right to suspend an internet domain name if, in its opinion, it is being used in a manner likely "to cause confusion to internet users." Nominet UK's practice is to look at the web site itself and make a judgement on whether it may cause confusion.

Nominet UK tries to assist resolving disputes of domain names but without prejudicing the parties' legal rights. It makes its views known in private, so its influence in recovering domain names for trademark owners is difficult to assess. Its dispute procedures assume willingness by the parties to accept informal procedures.

NSI practice

The difficulties in taking into account trademark issues at the time of registering a domain name were dramatically highlighted by the early practice of NSI, the US domain name registry, which adopted a trade-mark orientated policy when registering domain names. If a trademark owner could supply a trademark certificate certifying a trademark similar to a domain name, the NSI Registry would suspend the domain name until ownership issues were resolved. This seemingly innocuous rule led to difficulties and abuses.

Some trademark owners were quick to discover that certain foreign trademark offices were very willing to supply trademark registration certificates to order. A trademark certificate carrying a name similar to that of a registered domain name when placed before NSI was generally sufficient to trigger the removal of the domain name by NSI.

Difficulties also arose because under the trademark system it is possible for two separate businesses to hold separate trademark certificates for identical trademarks relating to different classes of goods, such as 'penguin' for books and biscuits.

In one dispute, Hasbro Inc. claimed the domain name www. perfection. com from a cyber-squatter on the grounds that it owned the trademark certificate 'perfection', but Hasbro was confounded when L'Oreal also produced a trademark certificate for 'perfection' and claimed rights to the domain name too. The dispute was settled before reaching the courts.

The NSI domain name practice of removing domain names on the strength of trademark registrations was heavily criticised. The procedure has now been dropped following the transfer of control of US domain names passing to ICANN.

A large number of gTLDs are owned by non-US citizens. In order to reflect the international ownership of gTLDs, ICANN requested the international body, World Intellectual Property Organisation (WIPO), to recommend the future management of the domain name system and, in particular, the control of cyber-squatting. Following ICANN's remit, WIPO prepared for ICANN a fast-track informal procedure for settling disputes between trademark owners and the owners of gTLD domain names.

ICANN/WIPO dispute resolution policy

WIPO's dispute procedures were adopted by ICANN as a part of its Uniform Domain Name Dispute Resolution Policy (UDRP). The policy took effect as from 1 January 2000 and applies to gTLDs ending in .com, .net and .org. The ICANN/WIPO's domain name dispute procedure provides a quick and informal means for trademark owners seeking to recover a domain name registration and is now being used effectively in connection with gTLDs.

A complainant must fulfil three conditions before attempting to recover a domain name. First, they must show that the disputed domain name is confusingly similar to their trademark (the trademark does not have to be registered). Second, they must supply reasons why the domain name holder should be regarded as having no rights to the name, and third, they must provide evidence that the domain name has been registered and is being used in 'bad faith'.

Indications of 'bad faith' include evidence to suggest that the domain name holder has primarily registered the domain name in order to sell it, or has registered the domain name to disrupt the complainant's business, or to attract internet users to the domain name site through confusion.

The dispute over the ownership of a domain name is referred to a WIPO panel, which must make a decision within 45 days. It is open to the parties to refer the panel's decision to the courts, but in most cases the order of the panel stands. Over 2,234 cases have been filed under the WIPO dispute procedure and as at 10 November 2000, 1,486 cases had been resolved. Total costs of each dispute are in the region of $1,000.

Examples of WIPO's hearings

The novelist Jeanette Winterson, author of *Oranges Are Not the Only Fruit*, challenged Cambridge academic Mark Hogarth, who had registered domain names using author's names including Julian Barnes, Peter Carey and Joanna Trollope, as well as Jeanette Winterson's. Mr Hogarth admitted that he had registered the writers' names in order to make money and his asking price for the transfer of the domain names was 3% of the gross book earnings for 1999.

The WIPO arbitrator had little difficulty in deciding that Mr Hogarth had acted in 'bad faith', as it was plain that the domain name owner had registered the names to demand money. He took a robust view that the authors' names were trademarks and accordingly ordered the domain name to be transferred to the author.

The key element for a trademark owner to succeed is evidence of 'bad faith'. In some cases the trademark owner may fail to meet this test, as in the case of Penguin Books, which could not persuade the WIPO panel to transfer to it the domain name www.penguin.org. The WIPO panel recognised that Penguin was an international trademark and well-known. However, the panel considered that the word 'penguin' had been honestly chosen by the domain name owner who used it as a nickname. The British rock star 'Sting' similarly failed to obtain www.sting.com because the name had been honestly chosen by a computer game player who used that name.

The importance of this WIPO procedure in reclaiming domain names should not be underestimated. Among the corporations that have won back their names under the WIPO rulings include Christian Dior, Nike, Reuters, Deutsche Bank and Microsoft.

Further developments

WIPO has made two further proposals to ICANN to assist trademark owners to recover gTLD domain names. These suggest there should be clear 'contact details' when domain names are registered, and a general 'exclusion order' should be maintained to protect famous names from being registered as domain names without the permission of trademark owners.

Domain name registries are advised to adopt best practice standards when registering domain names. Registries should collect accurate and reliable contact information about domain name owners and, if the information is shown to be unreliable, the domain name should be struck off. Accurate and clear records about the domain name owner may be vital when a trademark owner wishes to initiate legal proceedings against a domain name owner in the absence of the 'in rem' action introduced in the US.

The WIPO report recognises that famous and 'well-known' marks are 'special targets' for a variety of predatory and parasitic practices on the Internet. It recommends that ICANN adopts a policy to overcome the cyber-squatting of 'well-known' names by giving special rights to the owners of famous names to control domain names which may encroach on their international goodwill.

Another, and radical, measure is also proposed. A group of experts may on request determine whether a mark is 'famous' or 'well-known' and, if it is found to be so, the experts may make an 'exclusion order'. The order will prevent the registration of any domain name identical to the declared famous trademark.

In addition, the WIPO report proposes that, because domain names are often variations of well-known names, an 'exclusion order' should have the effect of placing on a domain name owner the burden of proving that a misleadingly similar domain name registration was made in good faith and justified.

The proposal envisages that a list of famous names having the benefit of an exclusion order would be maintained by WIPO. No definition of a famous name is offered, but WIPO's list of famous name criteria includes the requirement that the name should be well-known across a wide geographical area and across different classes of goods and services.

These WIPO proposals, if and when implemented, will be a formidable weapon for the owners of famous trademarks to control the future registration of domain names incorporating their names, because it will not be necessary to show 'bad faith' when making a complaint. The WIPO proposals would also place, for the first time, a responsibility on domain name registries to examine domain name applications to ensure that the terms of the 'exclusion orders' were being met – a burden, which some national registries may resist.

WIPO – further reforms?

Supporters of internet 'freedom' are becoming more vocal against WIPO's management of domain names. Despite such criticism, WIPO has recently announced further initiatives to control the abusive use of domain names.

WIPO intends to investigate the abusive registration of domain names beyond the cyber-squatting of trademarks. In particular, WIPO wants to consider the cyber-squatting of personality rights (such as the domain names of film stars), of trade names and geographical names, like Chateau Neuf du Pape. Whether WIPO's international discussions will lead to further inroads into the ownership of domain names only time will tell. But the influence of WIPO should not be underestimated.

Besides influencing the procedures of ICANN and the management of gTLDs it will probably not be long before WIPO establishes international procedures for domain name registries throughout the world.

WIPO has harmonised the international law of trademarks and copyright and the precedent has therefore been set for WIPO to be concerned with the international management of all domain names internationally. WIPO represents the interests of intellectual property owners, and the national domain name registries and the internet community may yet object to the erosion of the 'first-come, first-registered' principle.

In pursuing a policy of cancelling and removing domain names, WIPO may have unwittingly begun the difficult task of determining the rightful owners to a domain name. In addition, it may face invidious decisions, such as deciding which of two well-known names should own a domain name.

IP bias

Criticisms have been levelled at WIPO because its panels generally consist of IP lawyers who sympathise with trademark owners' interests. It is argued that a more diverse group of experts is needed.

Attention has also been drawn to the 'reverse highjacking' of domain names, when domain names are owned by individuals or small businesses without the financial resources to fight rich trademark owners who target a domain name. Balance, it is said, should be introduced into WIPO domain name disputes. Trademark owners should be made to post a financial bond before initiating legal challenges, strict time limits should be imposed for challenging the registration of domain names, and the short 10-day period for appealing against a panel decision should be reviewed.

The owner of a small English consultancy company called Chase Business Solutions Ltd registered the domain name www.chase.co.uk. Faced by a challenge from the rich Chase Manhattan Bank, the consultancy concluded that it had no option but to transfer its domain name to the international bank. Its revenge is to place on its internet site the message: "This is the awful story of how an obnoxious American investment bank has stiffed an innocent British IT company. It's a riveting tale of internet bullying..."

Public policy issues

The debate concerning domain names has concentrated on protecting private business interests, but public interest issues are likely to emerge. In the trademark world, geographical and descriptive names like 'Birmingham' and 'door' cannot be 'monopolised' by registration or trademarks. The extent to which such generic terms should be capable of being grabbed on the Internet is now being questioned

The issue has come to a head with geographical names because towns and villages have discovered that their names have been taken as domain names by persons quite unconnected with the town or village. The mayor of a French town took action to recover the domain name for his 'village', but was unsuccessful because of the honest motives of the domain name owner.

Barcelona City Council was more successful and won, through a WIPO arbitrator, the right to www.barcelona.com from barcelona.com Inc., a New York web business. WIPO ruled that the city had 'better rights' and 'more legitimate interests' in barcelona.com than the American company. The New York enterprise was considered to have acted in 'bad faith' as surfers 'would normally expect to reach some official body or representative of the city of Barcelona itself at barcelona.com'. WIPO also accepted the council's claim to sole right to provide tourist information about the city on the Internet.

Privacy interests are also being raised. A strong lobby believes that it should be possible to post information on a web site anonymously and opposes any requirement to provide contact addresses when registering domain names. WIPO has sought to placate this demand by suggesting that certain gTLDs might be reserved for those wishing not to complete contact addresses and so maintain their privacy.

Difficult questions concerning the jurisdiction of national courts remain outstanding, and with it the enforcement of court orders against domain name owners. Consider two direct mail companies having similar domain names registered under different country domains xxx.co.uk and xxx.co.ca., causing confusion to consumers. What jurisdiction does a court have, and will the court be able to enforce its judgement if directed to the company oversees? If a national court decides that a .com has been unfairly taken can it actually enforce the order in the US to require the NSI to remove the name?

Another problem for resolution is whether domain names are property and can be transferred freely like trademarks. In the US, courts have held that a domain name is a contractual right and that a domain name cannot be sold as bankrupt property. But in the UK, the Crown is happy to lay claim to 'orphan' domain names and to sell them on when the opportunity arises.

Future role of domain name registries

One risk of the direction being taken is that domain name registries might have to accept the adjudication and examination obligations associated with trademark offices. WIPO's minimum standards of adoption by domain name registries, for the recording of contact details about domain name owners, may be followed by further obligations on registries to examine the validity of domain names. If so, the question arises as to whether domain name registries can remain outside government interference and whether they should remain under private control.

The UK domain name registry has expressed unwillingness for its domains to be subject to WIPO's dispute resolution proposals, but national domain name registries may be unable to maintain independence from international developments. The demand and arguments for the central planning of all domain name registries may be difficult to resist.

The future

Unless, and until, the commercial value of domain names is removed, the friction between domain names and trademarks will continue as commercial enterprises seek to position and identify themselves in the public eye on the Internet.

ICANN has recommended the creation of further gTLDs but the addition of new domains is unlikely to resolve disputes. They will probably lead to trademark owners seeking to control the new domains by making a flush of further domain name registrations. Brand owners will lobby for the implementation of the WIPO 'exclusion order' proposals before the categories of domain name are extended.

The value of domain names, it is said, could be reduced by the arrival of new registration systems but the jury is out as to their effectiveness. A keyword system such as RealNames, which claims to provide a quicker system for finding domain names by typing in the name only of, for example Microsoft, will probably run into problems. Ultimately, a keyword system will have to decide whether an application for a domain name is distinctive to the applicant and will be required to choose between different and competing brand owners – and the shades of trademark office procedures begin to reappear.

Tim Berners-Lee, the accepted inventor of the web, in his book *Weaving the Web*, foresaw how the power of money and commercial interests would influence the internet and domain names. He wrote: "One problem is that the better domain names will wind up with the people or companies that have the most money, crippling fairness and threatening universality... It is essential that domain names be primarily owned by the people as a whole, and that they be governed in a fair and reasonable way by the people, for the people .... [The domain name system] shows how a technical decision to make a single point of reliance can be exploited for power and commercially for profit, breaking the technologies independence from these things, and weakening the web as a universal space."

The debate as to where the balance of power should lie in the management of the domain name system on the Internet looks set to continue for years to come. For the moment, brand owners are riding the trademark wave.

Hugh Brett interviews J. Scott Evans, chair of the Domain Name System Subcommittee of the International Trademark Association, and a shareholder in the IP law firm of Adams, Schwartz & Evans.

Q: A domain name is merely a string of numbers. Why should the first to register not own the name?

A: *A domain name is not merely a string of numbers. A domain name is an alphanumeric string, cross-referenced with an internet protocol – a series of numbers. Domain names were developed because internet protocols were cumbersome and difficult to remember. A domain name is a pneumonic device that makes information and web sites easier to find.*

In cyberspace, domain names serve the same function as trademarks and service marks in the real world. For this reason, it is extremely important that the 'first-come, first-served' atmosphere of the domain name registration system does not foster the abuse of IP rights. By enforcing mechanisms that prevent third parties from co-opting trademark and service mark rights in the 'first-come, first-served' registration system used for the domain name space, the internet community is helping to prevent consumer confusion and thwart profiteering.

Q: Do you think it is right to consider domains as IP?

A: *Most certainly. In many instances, domain names serve a source-identifying role in the virtual world similar to, if not identical to, the source-identifying role served by trademarks and service marks in the real world. A domain name can be a company's most valuable intangible asset. It is only appropriate that domain names are considered IP and afforded similar protections from abuse.*

Q: Who should be entitled to complain?

A: *Any party that feels it is being damaged by the use or registration of a domain name should feel free to complain. The national courts should be available for any aggrieved parties. As for the UDRP process, this should be limited to cases of 'bad faith' registration (cyber-squatting). Cyber-squatting is the one act that the majority of jurisdictions, that have considered the issue, have found violates the basic principals underlying IP – that a party seeking to exploit the trademark or service mark of another in 'bad faith' should not be allowed to continue to do so.*

Q: But requiring the transfer of a domain name is surely an interference with a property right?

A: *Certainly not. A determination that a party has registered a domain name in 'bad faith' establishes that the 'bad faith' domain name registrant has no property interest in the domain, in the same way that a thief has no property right in the watch stolen from the true owner. The transfer of a domain name from the 'bad faith' registrant to the rightful owner of the IP is no more draconian a remedy than an injunction preventing a trademark or service mark infringer or counterfeiter from continuing to use the offending mark.*

Q: Do you think it should be open to a trademark owner to question the status of a domain name at any time?

A: *Given the speed with which a domain name registration can be achieved, and the amount of time it may take to obtain a trademark registration in most jurisdictions, I think it would be inequitable to allow a 'bad faith' registrant to quickly register a domain name and not allow the trademark owner to bring a complaint until after its mark has achieved registration some 12 to 18 months down the road.*

Q: Why are the WIPO procedures proving to be very effective for brand owners?

A: *Allow me to clear up a common misconception. UDRP is not a WIPO policy and is not only applied by WIPO. UDRP is a dispute resolution policy adopted by ICANN and used by*

ICANN-accredited dispute resolution providers, of which WIPO is one.

UDRP has proved successful for many brand owners because of its design – it only applies where there is a demonstrable 'bad faith' on the part of the registrant. Many domain name registrants do not even respond to the complaint. Many arbitrators have used the failure to respond to justify inferring all facts in favour of the complainant. In my opinion, the fact that the UDRP is very narrowly tailored, and the fact that many registrants do not defend their domain name registration, accounts for the success brand owners have found under the policy.

Q: Has WIPO got any further plans to control the use of domain names and their transfer.

A: *WIPO does not develop domain name registration policy: this function is served by ICANN. ICANN has requested WIPO to conduct another consultative process to assist ICANN in developing policies regarding various issues related to the domain name system.*

Q: Do you think the rights to reclaim domain names should be extended to other classes of persons like owners of geographical descriptive terms and the inhabitants of towns. Should Oxford, England, prevail over Oxford, USA?

A: *I think the issue of personal names and geographic indications requires more study. I am hopeful that the second WIPO consultative process will assist ICANN in determining what, if any, policies should be adopted with regard to these variants of IP.*

Q: If national domain name registries, which in many cases are not under the control of government, are placed under a duty to examine trademarks (as in the case of 'well-known' names) will this not place unwelcome burdens on them?

A: *Not necessarily. Costs for this type of service can simply be passed onto the consumer.*

Q: Do you think a well-known name should have an 'objective' definition – say at least a minimum of trademark registrations.

A: *In my opinion, it would be far too difficult for any group to come up with any acceptable criterion for what is or is not a 'famous mark'. The better solution is well-reasoned application of the UDRP, and use of the national courts to protect trademark and service mark rights.*

Q: Can you see the present domain name registration system being replaced by another system?

A: *I hope that the domain name registration system could be revamped to lessen the tension between domain name registrations and trademarks. One practical solution is to abandon the 'first-come, first-served' premise.*

In the event that two domain names are registered that are identical, a directory could be created. An internet user seeking dominos.com would be linked to a directory listing all of the identical domains and a twenty-five word description of the information that exists on the web site hosted at the domain name (e.g. dominos.com – a premier franchiser for home delivery pizza stores located in Detroit, Michigan; dominos.com – a leading manufacturer of sugar products located in Sugarland, Texas; dominos.com – a site dedicated to the inspirational sound of the legendary Fats Domino.)

ICANN and the various registries would eliminate all incentive for cyber-squatting. Any infringement issues could be handled under standard trademark laws. I am sure this is not a popular solution because it would require registries and registrars to create an infrastructure to support such a system. Additionally, the 'first-come, first-served' rubric has been very profitable for registrars and registries because trademark owners and cyber-squatters alike know that they must move quickly to secure a domain name before another party registers the domain name.

This 'rush to the registrar' mentality has been extremely profitable for registrars and registries.

Q: Is reverse highjacking a legitimate worry?

A: *Yes. Unfortunately, any system will have cases where certain parties 'push the envelope'. I believe such cases are the rarity and, at least in the US, are seen for what they are by the courts. I hope that as case law around the world and the UDRP matures, that abuses of the system will become fewer and fewer.*

Paul Gosling interviews Robin Gross, lawyer for the Electronic Frontier Foundation

Q: Are you satisfied with the principle of domain name registration: 'first-come, first-registered'?

A: *Yes. It is an appropriate way to allocate domain names. I don't think there is any other way that would be workable. The idea that somebody with a federally registered trademark should get it is flawed in many ways, especially in trademark law. That should only happen if the domain name is identical to your trademark and will confuse consumers. Lots of different people can hold the trademark of the same name. You can't have a system where only one person is entitled to one name.*

Q: Is cyber-squatting a problem or a legitimate form of business?

A: *That depends on how you define cyber-squatting. If somebody who is unentitled to a name is deliberately using it to trade on others' goodwill to confuse consumers to look at their web site, then it's a problem. But simply sitting on a domain name which is somebody else's trademark is not enough.*

Q: What do you see as the main issues that domain names raise as they relate to trademarks?

A: *Freedom of expression principles are particularly threatened by the courts and the way ICANN dispute policies are appearing. These are extremely favourable to trademark registrants and not so favourable to individuals. There are many reasons why somebody would want to register a domain name.*

Q: Trademarks are national rights, and domain names are international. Does that pose problems?

A: *Yes. Different people can have the same trademarks overseas – even in the same country. Trademarks are issued federally/ nationally and so, in a lot of ways, trademarks will come into conflict with domain names. Somebody has to decide who gets domain names. 'First-come, first-served' is the only way to maintain fairness.*

Q: Is there an inevitable mismatch between trademarks and domain names, or do we simply need to agree a proper relationship between them?

A: *They are a mismatch. We should not think about them in the same way. Trade names are a property issue. They were originally not there to create a property for large organisations, but to protect consumers against confusion of origin of products and services. If you see a mark you have some reassurance where the goods come from.*

A domain name is simply an address like a telephone number, so people can find you. It is improper to claim that you have a property issue in a domain name that is separate from your trademark. It is not the same kind of IP.

Q: So are domain names a form of IP?

A: *No, I don't consider them IP in the traditional sense of IP, like copyright and patents, derived from the US constitution – a specific means for specific ends: an encouragement to create. The trademark is for consumer protection.*

Q: But a domain name can have a financial value, surely? So it becomes a form of property.

A: *It creates a value, of sorts. I guess you can think of it like a property issue. But it is inappropriate to analogise too much and think of it like personal property, because there are wider interests involved.*

Q: Is it right for a domain name to be tradable?

A: *Sure. Why not? It could be a commodity of sorts. It is valuable.*

Q: Who should have the right to complain about a registered name? And on what grounds?

A: *Somebody who is harmed by a particular domain name. So what do we mean by harmed? Simply using a domain name that is similar or identical to a trademark is not harm. If you have registered a domain name identical to a mark of another company with knowledge that people will be confused, and hope to sell goods or services to take advantage of that confusion, that is the type of harm which should lead to a complaint and get redress.*

Q: Do you feel that requiring the transfer of a domain name that infringes an existing trademark is an interference with a property right?

A: *It depends on what you mean about interference with rights of another. A lot of people will have legitimate rights to use a mark or a domain name. There is only one united.com, but there are lots of companies using 'United'. If you take that away from one person and give it to another, whose use is considered more legitimate. That is where I have a problem.*

Q: Do you believe that the ICANN/WIPO procedures are biased in favour of trademark and brand owners?

A: *That is a problem we have seen. They tend to favour trademark holders. There should be some kind of countervailing interest with other interests at the table. If you just leave it up to the companies with a property interest they will steer things in the direction that favours them, and that is what we have seen.*

Q: ICANN/WIPO procedures are surely designed for 'bad faith' registrations. Most disputes will need to go through the courts.

A: *I don't see the ICANN/WIPO policy as only being about 'bad faith'. There have been cases where people with legitimate interests in a domain name have lost them without there being 'bad faith'.*

Q: Will the planned extension of the number of top-level domain names exacerbate the conflict between domain names and trademarks, or reduce it?

A: *It really depends on how it is implemented and how it works in the real world. There could be problems. United Airlines under the new system could register every united.dot.whatever. It could come down to whoever runs to the registrar fastest. Just creating a whole new area of things that can be propertised doesn't resolve the underlying problem that there are a lot of legitimate interests in the same name.*

Q: Should national domain name registries have a duty to examine trademarks or 'well-known' names before they approve a domain name?

A: *No.*

Q: Are they currently capable of doing this?

A: *No. In addition to having competing trademarks, there are also common law trademarks. The level of searching and figuring out whether anyone else is using this word is too onerous for people just supposed to register names. What does a trademark represent? What are the other users [of a trademark] doing? What would [the domain name applicant] be doing? Would the consumer be confused? Maybe it is currently out of their line, but maybe it is something they would do in the future?*

It would be a really big mistake.

Q: Do you think a well-known name should have an 'objective' definition.

A: *I don't think well-known names or not-so-well-known names should matter in the domain names system. McDonalds has a well-known trademark. But trying to provide special protection for them steps on other interests that are legitimate – people who use that word for some reason. Their rights would be squashed.*

Q: Does the debate over the relationship between trademarks and domain names tell us anything about the relevance of traditional IP to the web? Does the web change the rules of IP?

A: *I don't think the web changes the rules. It makes the current rules unworkable. Rules will change when the laws themselves change. The fact that much of the traditional IP rules and regimes don't fit into cyberspace is a good sign that they are not working and they need some kind of change.*

Q: Would you like to see the present domain name registration system replaced by another system?

A: *If we had a system that did not give such deference to large corporations with registered federal marks, that would be a step in the right direction. Having a procedure that the average guy on the street could understand, and could apply his rights to, would be good. There is no choice but to use a lawyer and the average person is not in a position to defend his domain name, and that has got to be changed.*

Q: Is reverse highjacking a legitimate worry?

A: *I think this is a worry. We see lots of corporations taking away the domain names of people just because they have a trademark. Until we throw the lawyers out, I don't know how to proceed.*

Chapter Four
Patents and the web: friends or foes?
By Richard Poynder

In the beginning

Patents have a long history. In medieval times, the granting of exclusive rights or 'monopolies' by the sovereign was a more popular way to raise money than taxation. The first law that granted exclusive rights, for limited periods, to the makers of inventions as a conscious form of economic policy was in Venice in 1474.

In 1624, the English Parliament passed the 'Statute of Monopolies'. This allowed monopolies to be granted to inventions for 14 years (the duration of two training periods for craft apprentices). The first US patent laws were enacted by Congress in 1790.

There have been many subsequent changes to patent laws around the world, and some differences remain between national and regional patent offices as to how patents are granted and what constitutes patentability. However, there is now a general consensus that patents can be granted for the invention of any new and useful art, machine, manufacture, or composition of matter, or any new and useful improvement of such things.

The original English approach – later emulated in the American Constitution – was to place the emphasis on the benefits of new inventions to society at large. This assumed a bargain between society and the inventor that provided mutual advantage. Society got the benefits of the invention and the inventor got a limited monopoly in which to exploit it commercially. This tension between the rights of individuals and society is a recurrent theme in many of today's discussions about the web and IP.

The power of monopolies has tended to encourage inventors to turn to the patent system for support, often controversially. One hundred years ago critics questioned whether agricultural inventions could be protected, on the grounds that agriculture was not an industry. Twenty years ago it was argued that granting pharmaceutical patents would be unethical and, today, the biotechnology industry finds itself at the centre of the so-called 'patenting of life' debate.

Nevertheless, as a general rule, the patent system has tended to absorb each new industry, although governments have imposed limitations on the extent to which the patent system can be used.

Patents in the age of the web

Inevitably, the web has created its own controversy with critics opposing the patenting of web technologies and practices. Again the question has been raised, is the Internet sufficiently different and unusual that its techniques and technologies should be seen as outside the scope of the patent system?

Traditionalists point to the old controversies that surrounded earlier 'new industries' and insist that the patent system will adapt to the web – or vice versa – and should therefore play a central role in furthering innovation. Critics argue that patents are inappropriate in cyberspace and rather than furthering innovation they could impede it. The Internet, they claim, is special.

Some background: an American story

The Internet has been the trigger for one of the most hotly-contested debates over the role of the patent system since patenting began. The origins of today's controversy lie in earlier conflicts and developments and, like most things connected with the Internet, the debate has its roots in the US.

In the 1980s, US computer chip manufactures found themselves under serious competitive threat from Japanese manufacturers. By 1987, points out Fred Warshofsky in his book *The Patent Wars,* "there were only two American companies still making the most widely used memory chips, the Dynamic Random Access Memory chip. One was a small producer in Idaho called Micron Technologies. The other was Texas Instruments."

Faced with mounting economic pressure from new foreign competitors US politicians, and the courts, underwent a conversion. Where previously patents had been viewed as over-monopolistic, it became accepted that strong IP rights were vital for fostering innovation. In 1980 the Bayh-Dole Act was enacted, which for the first time permitted federal agencies to grant patent rights to non-profit and federally funded research centres. The 1980s also saw the US Supreme Court reverse its previous stance that patents were inherently anti-competitive, and the relaxation of federal anti-trust laws to corporate joint ventures in R&D.

Above all, it was the creation by the US Congress of a new, specialised, Court of Appeals of the Federal Circuit (CAFC) in 1982 that changed the patent landscape in the US. Prior to the creation of the CAFC, argue Kevin Rivette and David Kline in *Rembrandts in the Attic,* 75% of patent claims were denied by US courts. After the CAFC was created this reversed, with around 75% being upheld, and substantially larger damage awards being levied against patent infringers.

In the light of this more sympathetic climate, Texas Instruments (TI) filed a complaint, in 1986, with the International Trade Commission against eight Japanese companies and one Korean semiconductor maker, charging infringement of ten of their US patents. The action was successful, forcing infringers to agree licensing arrangements with TI. "Like the Battle of Concord, it too was a 'shot heard round the world'," quips Mr. Warshofsky.

But it was Polaroid's historic patent victory against Kodak in 1986 that brought home the sea change that had taken place. Following Polaroid's $1bn damage suit against Kodak for patent infringement, Kodak had to dismantle its entire instant photography business.

Suddenly owning and enforcing patents was viewed as a vital part of the corporate landscape and, consequently, many US companies have come to view their IP portfolio as their most important asset. By 1992, TI was earning $391m in royalties, compared to an operating income of just $274m. IBM earns a phenomenal $1bn a year in licensing royalties from its patent portfolio.

The battleground shifts to software and 'business methods'

The second significant development behind today's controversy was the explosive growth of the US software industry. As the source of greatest value in computing shifted from hardware to software, so software companies became concerned at the lack of protection for their sophisticated and highly expensive products. Copyright and trade secrets alone were no longer sufficient.

The difference, points out Axel Casalonga, a European Patent Attorney at Bureau D A Casalonga-Josse, in Paris, is that where "copyright protects only the code of a software program, not the idea behind it" a patent protects "the main inventive idea within the software."

As a result, increasing efforts were made to have software accepted as patentable matter, with success coming in 1981, in the shape of a US Supreme Court decision – *Diamond v. Diehr*. This ruled for the first time that software could be patented. But the most radical shift in US legal practice concerning patentability came in 1998, with a dramatic decision of the CAFC – *State Street Bank & Trust Co v. Signature*

Financial Group Inc. This concluded that it was also possible to patent business methods.

These two legal decisions unleashed a flood of patenting activity in the US and as a consequence, some argue, it is now possible to take any known business method from the real world, build the process into software, apply that process to the Internet and then patent it.

Today, this issue is a source of considerable debate in the US, and, as we shall see, although the debate has its origins in the US it will affect Europe and Asia too.

Show me the 'prior art'

The patenting of software raises several practical issues. The software industry had relied on copyright and trade secrets alone during the first 40 years of its development, and many of the inventive steps and untrodden byways that software engineers took have never entered the public domain. This shortage of 'prior art' makes it very difficult for patent examiners to assess the novelty of software patent applications.

A controversial software patent, granted in 1993, to multimedia company Compton's New Media exemplifies the problem. When the company startled the audience of a Las Vegas computer convention by announcing that it had been awarded a US patent covering the search technology for running computer-based multimedia presentations, there was a storm of protest. The implication was that any company selling multimedia products in the US would now have to pay between 1-3% royalty to Compton's on every item it sold.

A year later, however, the US Patent and Trademark Office (USPTO) announced that after "exhaustive re-examination" of the claim it had decided to reverse its earlier decision. With software lying at the heart of e-commerce patents, incidents like this are grist to the mill of the critics of web-based patents.

Too broad

Nevertheless, as a result of these legal changes, a rapidly growing collection of highly controversial web-based patents now haunts the USPTO. Many of them, critics insist, are as inappropriate as the Compton's New Media patent.

Massachusetts-based Open Market, for instance, has been granted several patents that, some claim, could potentially allow it to demand royalties from almost any company engaged in e-commerce. These include a patent on a secure, real-time payment method using debit and credit cards, one covering electronic shopping carts, and another on a technique for analysing how users browse web content.

Likewise, Sightsound.com claims to have been granted a patent that covers the sale of any digital audio or video recording over the Internet. As such it is currently suing CDNow, one of the most successful music sites on the web. The company has also written to a number of other prominent music sites demanding royalties on every sale that involves downloading music to a customer.

One complaint is that many of these new patents are too broad in scope. "We are seeing some very, very broad claims on patents governing the Internet," says Cary Sherman, senior executive for music systems at the Recording Industry Association of America (RIAA), "which could have a tremendous impact on the ability of the new medium to develop."

E-commerce is different?

If the patenting of software presents challenges, the sanctioning of business method patents has created a far more puzzling conundrum.

Novelty is perhaps the most contentious issue. When Cybergold (subsequently acquired by MyPoints.com) was issued a patent on pay-per-view advertising (where users are rewarded for looking at internet-based advertisements), many questioned its novelty. This is a criticism which Cybergold's CEO, Nat Goldhaber, roundly dismisses. "When I explained what we were doing to one of the leading men in American advertising, he told me our business model was so innovative that he would have to go back and re-learn the business," he responds.

Also frequently cited in this regard is Priceline.com which, amongst other things, claims to have patent rights on internet-based 'reverse auctions' – where buyers propose a price for a product or service and sellers bid to supply it.

One problem, concludes Seth Shulman, author of *Owning the Future*, is that these "new patent rights often function like needless toll-booths demanding royalty fees on everyone in an industry or, worse still, like roadblocks that deter would-be competitors. Far from their original intent, these patents deter innovation."

In response, Sightsound.com CEO, Scott Sander, insists that all patent owners are asking for is the same reward that any inventor could expect. "Sony and Philips received a royalty for each compact disc that was sold while their patents on CD technology were in force," he says. "We're seeking the same right."

But, says Mr Sherman, e-commerce is different because it requires such a wide range of technologies. "You may have to use compression technologies, watermarking technologies, encryption technologies, clearing house technologies – all of which could be an essential component of a digital distribution system," he says. "Paying royalties on all these technologies adds up, and represents a significant cost factor."

Rembrandts in the attic

With the huge value now placed on IP there are also concerns that companies are starting to mine their patent portfolios in order to opportunistically leverage them in cyberspace. This technique was promoted in Kevin Rivette's and David Kline's book, *Rembrandts in the Attic*. As the name implies, the authors argue that many companies are sitting on hugely valuable IP that could reap them significant financial rewards if better exploited.

When, in June 2000, BT announced that it had a US patent on the hyperlinking technology that lies at the heart of the web, it was a neat demonstration of this thesis. Whether this patent will prove enforceable in the courts has yet to be established but one of the most interesting aspects of this incident is that BT 'discovered' its hyperlink patent accidentally 11 years after it was granted. The patent in question had been created for a long-defunct videotext system, Prestel, which only adds to the irony.

The web community reacted angrily, with critics arguing that it is beyond common sense that the patent system should be used to exploit patents, from an earlier technology, in cyberspace. Besides, how could a company claim to have invented the concept of the hyperlink before the web even existed?

"Someone better tell Ted Nelson about this development," commented a wag on the ZDNet bulletin board. "Since Xanadu [the hyperlinking project founded by Ted Nelson in 1960] had been in development 20 plus years before BT claims it 'invented' hyperlinks."

1-Click: the web fights back

But the greatest controversy so far has been sparked by the granting of Amazon.com's patent on 1-Click shopping. When it was announced that Amazon.com was suing barnesandnoble.com for infringing this patent the web community again complained violently.

As part of the ensuing campaign of protest, Tim O'Reilly, open source software activist and founder of O'Reilly & Associates, published an open letter to Amazon.com's CEO, Jeff Bezos. "We believe that the rapid innovation of the world wide web and internet platform that has created so much new value for the public (as well as for Amazon and its shareholders) will be choked off if companies take the short-sighted route of filing patents on commonly accepted and obvious techniques in an attempt to keep competitors from using them." he said, adding: "Ill-advised patents and other attempts to limit the use of web technology for private advantage have put the whole software development and standards process into a precarious state."

Startled at the virulence of the reaction, and facing a boycott of his business, Bezos responded by publishing an open letter on Amazon.com's web site. To everyone's surprise, however, he confided that after giving the matter a lot of thought he too agreed that: "it's possible that the current rules governing business method and software patents could end up harming all of us – including Amazon.com and its many shareholders."

Patent laws now needed to recognise, Bezos explained, that business method and software patents are fundamentally different to other kinds of patents. As a result, he suggested, such patents should have a much shorter lifespan than the current 17 years. "I would propose three to five years," he said, adding that there should also be a short period for public comment before a patent is issued "to give the internet community the opportunity to provide prior art references." He concluded, however, that "it would not be right" for Amazon.com to unilaterally give up its patents – although he promised the company would be careful in how it used its patents in future.

Traditionalists, however, don't agree, insisting that the rules are no different in cyberspace than they are in the real world.

Up the ladder of abstraction

So what is at issue? What is inherently problematic, suggests Mr Shulman, is the "highly conceptual nature of many of today's patents." As he explains: "Our intellectual property system thrived in the mechanical age, providing patent protection for tangible machines, like new toasters. In the US system, 19th century inventors were even required to make prototype models to receive a patent. Today we have moved unrecognisably higher up the ladder of abstraction. Instead of allotting protections on new toaster designs, today's patents more often afford exclusive rights on conceptual terrain akin to the idea of making toast."

In an article published on the Derwent Information web site in 1999, the then newly-appointed US Commissioner of Patents & Trademarks, Todd Dickinson, disputed this line of argument. "Software patents may seem 'different' from patents over physical objects, but the patent system's principles of novelty, non-obviousness, and utility work the same in this technology as in any other." he stated, adding: "Software patents are basically patents claiming a process, for which the US has been granting patents throughout its history."

Nevertheless, as we have seen, the patenting of software does pose practical 'prior art' issues. In addition, say critics, the sheer number of patent applications, combined with a shortage of patent examiners, is putting huge pressure on the system. More importantly, says Greg Aharonian, the infamous patent buster who runs the *PATNEWS* mailing list, the USPTO is simply not equipped to assess the validity of patents. "They have no idea what is going on in the industry," he told the web publication *NetworkWorldFusion* in June 2000.

In 1999, Commissioner Dickinson was not prepared to accept this, staunchly defending both the novelty and breadth of US patents. He explained: "We have a highly skilled group of patent examiners with a technical background that matches up very well with the kind of technologies they are seeing – and we think we issue patents of an appropriate breadth."

He added: "A lot of commentators have worried that patents will issue on business methods that have been used for years. But that is not going to happen because if they have been used for years, and publicly, then a patent cannot be issued as the method is not novel."

A patent flood

What Commissioner Dickinson was unable to deny was that the current popularity of the patent system is creating real problems for the USPTO. Quite apart from the flood of new software and business method patents, the increased emphasis on 'intangible assets' in the knowledge economy has caused an explosion of patent applications, with companies increasingly focused on 'sweating' their patent portfolios, both by active management of patent portfolios, as well as a new patent-everything-that-moves attitude.

The consequence is that, in 1998, the number of US patents issued reached nearly 155,000 – a 33% increase over 1997. In 1999, this had grown to 289,000. In terms of software patents alone, while there were a manageable 1,600 software patents issued by the USPTO annually in the 1990s, by 1997 this had reached 13,000, last year's figure had grown to 22,500.

In support of the current patenting philosophy in the US, many commentators argue that while there may be signs that there is a temporary problem, there is no evidence of a fundamental mismatch between the web and the traditional patent system.

Many will concede, however, that the sheer speed with which the web is developing poses a significant challenge for the USPTO. "Like everybody else, the US Patent Office has been caught out by the Internet," says Chuck Williams, chief scientist of Cylink, a Californian company that has itself been granted a number of patents covering encryption. "It simply doesn't have time to learn what makes sense, and what doesn't."

Reviewing the situation

Beset on all sides, the USPTO announced a review initiative in Spring 2000, with the stated aim of overhauling the way it reviews web patents. "The number of patent applications related to computer-implemented business methods continues to grow, doubling in the last year, demonstrating that business method patents play an important role in this growing industry," said Commissioner Dickinson. "In an effort to enhance the quality of the examination of business method patent applications, the USPTO is interested in working to identify ways to improve the current business operations and solve business methods related issues."

As part of this process the USPTO held a roundtable meeting on the topic on July 27th 2000, in Arlington, Virginia. An event, comments Sam Adler, editor-in-chief at *Corporate Intelligence,* that at times generated "more heat than light", and during which "Amazon's patented 1-Click system came up again and again."

Long-time critic of the USTPO, Greg Aharonian, however, throws cold water on expectations that the review will achieve the necessary changes. "It is pointless for the PTO to try to improve the quality of issued software/internet/business method patents until it gets a better grasp of the current [low] quality of such patents," he commented in *PATNEWS.* "Without measurements of past quality to benchmark quality measurements in the future, especially after the introduction of reforms, you can make no progress."

Time will tell how successful the USPTO proves in silencing its critics. As we shall see in chapter six, the political agenda may in any case force its hand.

But what does the debate mean for the rest of the world?

US seeks to export its model

Until recently it was assumed that the e-commerce patent controversy was essentially a US issue. In Europe software has not historically been deemed patentable. Article 52 of the European Patent Convention (EPC) expressly prohibits the patenting of software. Nor is it generally accepted that business methods can be patented.

However, given today's global economy, and the lack of boundaries on the Internet, US companies want to extend the patenting of software and business methods beyond the shores of the US, with the aim of ensuring that their IP has the same protection abroad as at home.

Simultaneously, the US government has exerted pressure on other national and regional patent offices to adopt the US model, notably through the World Trade Organisation (WTO). In particular, it has pursued an aggressive IP policy through the WTO's Trade-Related

Aspects of Intellectual Property Rights (TRIPs) agreement, negotiated during the Uruguay Round of the GATT Accord.

By making membership of the WTO an indispensable ticket to economic development, and by making TRIPs a required obligation of WTO members, the current system, argued academic lawyer Peter Gerhart in the *European Intellectual Property Review*, provides "the institutional machinery for continually refining and unifying intellectual property standards, for making the property less costly to acquire and protect, and ultimately for providing global rights and remedies."

In other words, argue critics, the US is using the mechanism of the WTO, along with the World Intellectual Property Organisation (WIPO), to highjack current harmonisation initiatives to forcefully export its IP system to the rest of the world.

In fairness, suggests Bob Hart, chairman of the Computer Technology Committee of the UK's Chartered Institute of Patent Agents (CIPA), European companies played a role here, too. Fearful that they will be at a disadvantage to their US competitors unless they have comparable IP protection, they have exhorted their national governments to adopt the US approach. "There is a lot of pressure coming from large European companies like Siemens and Philips to have Europe also conform to the State Street Bank decision," says Mr. Hart.

Caught in this pincer movement, Europe has been finding it hard to resist. Member states of the EPC initially conceded to the principle of replacing Section 52 of the EPC with wording agreed during the Uruguay Round of the GATT Accord, which would have rubber stamped the patenting of software in Europe too. However, this action was postponed in November 2000, following the decision of the EC to engage in a public consultation process, on the merits of patenting computer-implemented inventions.

On 21 November 2000, in the wake of the news that the EC had initiated a consultation process, the Munich Diplomatic Conference of all twenty states of the EPC agreed not to remove the software exclusion, pending further consultations with interested parties. This reversed a

10-9 vote at the EPO Administrative Council held in September 2000 to remove the exclusion.

Europe holds to the 'technical effect'

In fact, many argue that the European Patent Office (EPO) has been granting software patents for a number of years – with companies able to sidestep the restriction of Article 52 on the grounds that patents can be granted on software if it is an integral part of a new machine. This is fulfilled if software, such as an operating system, controls the functions of that machine.

But the official view in Europe today remains that while the principle of the patenting of software may indeed be eventually accepted, the patenting of business methods is probably a step too far. Europe believes it has got the balance right on this issue.

The difference between the European patent system and the US system, says Mr. Hart, is the European requirement for a 'technical effect'. He explains: "So far as the EPO is concerned, only those inventions that provide a technical contribution can be patentable. This is very different to the US position because if you look at the interpretation of the State Street case all that is required is that inventions are technically implemented: they don't have to have a 'technical effect'."

In other words, he adds: "In the US, so long as it is technically implemented, the invention does not have to have a technical contribution. In Europe, on the other hand, you have to have a technical justification for the invention, for instance, that it speeds things up, provides a bridge, or manipulates data with less steps than were previously necessary, and so on."

Stalemate

For the moment we face stalemate, with the US and Europe continuing to approach the matter from different perspectives. "We are not likely to find harmonisation in the short term," suggests Dai Rees, director of one of the departments responsible for examination of computer-related inventions at the EPO. "Although undoubtedly there will be a lot of pressure from the Americans: on the other hand, the Americans may feel some pressure in return."

Meanwhile, there is a growing tide of dissent over both business method and software patents in Europe. Open source advocates at the EuroLinux Alliance are so opposed to the issue of software patents that in 2000 they organised an online petition against the introduction of software patenting into Europe. Within weeks, they claimed, over 20,000 people had signed it.

And, in an open letter to BT about its hyperlink patent, the Alliance commented: "You have supplied us with a brilliant proof on the absurdity of software patents at a time where European legislators are poised to legalise them in Europe."

One of those who signed the EuroLinux Alliance petition, Klaus Weidner of Munich's WMP GmbH, commented to *Wired News* that patents are "supposed to promote invention and progress, but software patents would have the opposite effect." The reason: "being able to create interoperability between programs requires either open standards or reverse-engineering of protocols or file formats."

Weidner's fear is that access to, or alteration of, software coding would be prohibited by software patents, and that companies with a large market share would be able to stifle competition.

A resolution of the issue?

In the meantime the Japanese Patent Office (JPO) is also reviewing the situation and is in the process of revising its current Examination Guideline. At the time of publication details of this were expected to be published on the JPO homepage in the near future, with an English translation following shortly after. "Japan is interesting in this respect," comments Mr. Rees. "We don't yet know in what direction they will go over this."

Many believe that Europe holds the key to resolving the issue in the long-term. "I think we may find that the EPO will act as a stabilising factor," says Mr. Williams, "if only because it may make its decision a year after the US patent office – and a year is a long time on the web."

The hope is that if Europe and Asia do not adopt the principle of patenting business methods, then the impact of many of the controversial e-commerce patents will be confined to the US. But there are reasons for doubting this.

Professor Richard Stern, of George Washington University Law School, says that, even if Europe and Asia decide not to follow the US example, companies elsewhere will still be affected. "It depends how the patents are written," he says, "but you would be surprised what kind of extraterritorial reach US patents can have. Consider a European firm conducting e-commerce transactions with US-based customers in a way that infringes a US patent. If that patent is a method patent, it is possible to file an infringement suit against that company in the US on the theory that the product is being shipped to the US after being made by a process patented in the US." In other words, the legal reach of a US patent can be extended across the globe.

"A European company could infringe a US patent simply by having a customer complete an electronic form over the web, even though it never sets foot outside its own country," adds Stern. "I consider this an irrational over-extension of US law, but the bottom line is that even if many of the controversial e-commerce patents are issued only in the US, the nature of the Internet means that their influence will be felt globally."

Future scenarios

What, then, does the future hold? Clearly this is a global issue. The fear of the radicals is that the wholesale patenting of web technologies will eventually grind the network to a halt. Companies will be unable to operate because of prohibitive licensing demands while patent offices and the courts will be swamped with patent claims and counter claims, and companies will waste billions of dollars fighting pointless legal actions.

The traditionalists argue that the current teething problems will recede and the web will function better by providing innovators with incentives. "In the final analysis patenting will be as important to the Internet as in any other field," insists Mr. Goldhaber. "In other words, people will be willing to take bigger risks and make bigger investments because they know their investments are protected."

Even if that were true, respond the radicals, unless the rules are changed the web will rapidly become off-limits to all but the largest enterprises. Smaller companies, they say, will simply not compete in the harsh atmosphere of multiple patented web technologies. There is, says Philip Sargent, CEO of UK-based web-database development company Metaweb, "definite and widespread" evidence that software patents are used mostly as bargaining counters in takeover negotiations and in "bludgeoning smaller companies without large legal staff."

He adds: "A small company has only a couple of people who understand the innovative technology and can articulate it – this is precisely the skill needed to sell new innovative ideas to early adopters. Using up these people in lengthy discussions with lawyers is the worst thing a small company can do. Patents are also slow and expensive – in money, as well as time – and suit large companies' time-scales, but not those of small companies."

Traditionalists counter that the patent system will level the playing field, providing small companies with the means to stand up to major corporations. "Today if you can obtain an internet method or process patent you've got a fighting chance against the big guys – in the same way that historically if you obtained a new method or process patent for making steel you had a chance against Andrew Carnegie," says Mr. Sander.

Eventually, suggest the radicals, it will be necessary for governments to intervene and take into public ownership those patents deemed too valuable to leave in the hands of private corporations. "Like roads, public lands or public libraries, pooled knowledge assets must be made freely accessible and protected within a framework that preserves their integrity," says Mr. Shulman. "In this sense, some types of knowledge constitute a shared infrastructure – or 'infostructure' – that belongs to all of us. As we build a global economy for the 21st century, we need a new way to think about this conceptual commons."

Herein, perhaps, lies the nub of the debate – and a point that harks back to the principles that lay at the heart of the early patent laws. How does society continue to maintain a proper balance in sharing the benefits of new inventions between the rights of individual inventors and the rights of society?

Is traditional IP being leveraged in the web economy today in such a way that balance remains equitable, or is it being disrupted by the Internet? And what is government's responsibility in maintaining, or restoring, that balance? We shall return to this in chapter six.

Richard Poynder interviews Drummond Reed, chief technology officer, OneName Inc.

Q: In 1999, your company – formerly Intermind Inc. – announced that it had a patent on a technology that the World Wide Web Consortium (W3C) was intending to use in the new Platform for Privacy Preferences (P3P) internet standard. You attracted considerable controversy when you published details of the royalties you expected for that technology. What's happened since then?

A: *There was a complete management change at the company, the policy was reversed, and we subsequently wrote to the W3C indicating that we were now happy to provide a royalty-free licence for our technology. As it happens, P3P 1.0 would not have violated the claims of our patent as the specification was eventually scaled back.*

Q: What does your patent cover?

A: *Our technology is called 'web agents', and it's based on exchanging objects to control and automate communications. We are just now introducing the first global standard for web agent technology, called XNS, or Extensible Name Service. XNS is the next logical step in the development of a truly universal address system for the web, beyond the Domain Name Service (DNS) – although it isn't going to replace DNS. It is a 'higher level' naming service that adds many other powerful new auto-mated data exchange and linking services.*

Q: How does this relate to privacy?

A: *Privacy is 'built in' to XNS data exchange – every single inter-change between two XNS web agents results in an XML-encoded, legally binding privacy contract. This type of data exchange control is just one of twelve different control types that are specifically covered in our patent specifications. Web agents can also negotiate security, encoding, forwarding, and a number of other communications functions.*

Q: What do your experiences with your patent tell us about traditional IP and the web?

A: *If you have a patent that covers something that needs to be standardised in order to be widely adopted – and there are more and more internet technologies where that has to happen – then it is going to have to become part of the infrastructure in order for the solution to work.*

Q: So asserting a web patent is problematic?

A: *What people are finding is that trying to put up a patent in front of the rapidly flowing river of the web is like trying to dam it. But the river is so powerful that it will simply work around you, or wash over you. We were the first company that said we are not going to contribute IP royalty-free to a W3C standard. And look what happened!*

Q: Many argue that patents like yours underline a growing conflict between the traditional IP system and the web. Is there a general problem with internet-related patents?

A: *In the US right now there is a problem with the number of internet patents being issued, and the quality of those patents.*

Q: Is this a management problem, or evidence that patenting is inappropriate for web technologies?

A: *A management problem. It seems to be a combination of the sheer number of applications, and examiners without sufficient training or resources. In addition, they don't appear to have access to a knowledge base of applicable software or networking 'prior art', or the time to search 'prior art' resources properly.*

Q: Yours is a software patent. The main controversy surrounds business method patents. Are there problems here?

A: *I do agree that business methods that simply capture the set of computer steps for accomplishing a business task – and where there is no novelty in the way that the process is automated – should not qualify for patent protection. However, a number of the business method patents that have been issued would meet that test.*

Q: Nevertheless, you are now offering your technology on a royalty-free basis. So where's the benefit to OneName of owning this patent?

A: *We decided that the key thing is to find a business model in which – rather than earn royalties or direct licensing fees – we can gain leverage, or business advantage, by licensing our IP to advance a standard.*

Q: What does this mean in practice?

A: *One of the big advantages that certain types of services or standards can have is that they promote interoperability. We are using our IP to that effect, specifically through freely giving licences to anyone who wants to use out technology – so long as they agree to maintain one interoperable standard for XNS.*

Q: So how will you earn revenue from your IP?

A: *We will provide services. This will include various web agent-based services for individuals and businesses. Essentially it is a White Pages/Yellow Pages model: largely free to individuals, but businesses pay for these services.*

Q: Given that everyone will be able to use your technology for free what benefit will you obtain from inventing the technology? The companies you license XNS to could become major competitors, and take business away from you?

A: *That could happen. But the best model for us is to open it up in this way. The advantage we have is being a first mover. The advantage to everyone is that we will use our intellectual property rights (IPR) very specifically to maintain interoperability. This will neutralise the advantage of much larger companies, such as Microsoft or IBM, who might otherwise try and make it proprietary.*

Q: Not many patent owners will take this approach. With so many web patents being granted, those wanting to do business on the web may face such a barrage of royalty demands that the web's development could be slowed down. Right?

A: *I don't agree. I strongly believe market forces will always work as the appropriate licensing model, and that's also the most efficient solution. It's supply and demand. IP owners won't design licenses or charge royalty rates that would be prohibitive to potential licensees.*

Q: What about the most controversial e-commerce patents – those granted to companies like Sightsound.com, Open Market and Priceline.com. Are you saying these patents are not as harmful as many claim?

A: *When people allege that, I challenge them to point to one patent that has become a real problem in the way you imply. While I don't say there is no problem here, I do believe it is over-hyped. Take the most visible internet patent of all, Amazon's 1-Click patent. You can see how the internet community has stood up to Amazon over this. And to date I don't think Amazon has asserted its patent against anyone but a direct competitor. Nor do I expect it to.*

Q: So you don't see any need for action by governments or patent offices?

A: *No. The beauty of the invisible hand of the market is that it allows the system to evolve, and smooth out the wrinkles. Most importantly, it will allow the evolution of the web to continue at an extremely rapid pace.*

Q: I understand what you say about market forces, but given the main thrust of those market forces today, including the importance of interoperability, and the power of the web community to challenge corporate expectations, does this not imply that traditional IP is of little relevance on the web?

A: *The important word here is 'traditional'. I don't think the traditional business model of demanding and obtaining royalties is going to end up being applicable in many cases on the web.*

Q: So the Internet has fundamentally changed the rules?

A: *Yes, but changed the rules of licensing and of leveraging IP, not the rules for obtaining it.*

Q: So there remains value in owning IP in the web economy, but it may be necessary to find alternative ways of exploiting that ownership?

A: *Yes. I can tell you from my own experience that if we didn't have any IP we wouldn't even exist today. We have been told many times by our investors that their investment has been sustained by our development and ownership of IP, and in the business model we are pursuing because of it*

Q: So traditional IP is still very definitely relevant in the web economy?

A: *Yes. The fundamental rules are the same. What is different is the business model. How you leverage your IP is dramatically different. That is where we are going to see the really big impact.*

Richard Poynder interviews Dai Rees, Director, Directorate 2.2.01, European Patent Office

Q: What is Directorate 2.2.01?

A: *We are one of four departments at the EPO that deal with the examination of computer-related inventions. We have two main focuses: one is computer architecture, both in the hardware and software sense; and the other is applications.*

Q: There is a lot of controversy in the US right now over the patenting of web-related technologies. Does the EPO believe that internet-related patents are problematic?

A: *We are certainly doing a lot of thinking about the issue, and making sure we have a reasonably coherent and clear position.*

Q: The patents at the centre of the debate in the US tend to be software and/or business method patents. It was thought that Europe was about to remove its long-standing prohibition on the patenting of software. But there has been a delay?

A: *Right. It was expected that the reference to programs for computers as not being patentable subject-matter would be removed from the European Patent Convention at the Diplomatic Conference in November 2000, and that in all probability the proposed directive from the European Commission/Parliament would support this move.*

Q: What's changed?

A: *In the meantime, opponents of software patents have mounted a very successful lobbying effort with national governments and the EC. This has introduced some doubt in their minds as to the wisdom of the move, or at least that there is a consensus.*

Q: So what is likely to happen?

A: *It is still likely that the amendment will be made, but there is now also a fair chance that it will be at least delayed until 2001, when European governments have had time to think about their positions more thoroughly.*

Q: And business method patents? Can they be patented in Europe?

A: *Currently a pure business method cannot be patented in Europe. However, a business method that is implemented in a technology is not necessarily excluded from patentability.*

Q: Can you explain what that means?

A: *If the EPO had existed 100 years ago Alexander Graham Bell might have come to us and said that by inventing the telephone he had created a new way of doing business – as talking to people is an improvement over having to send telegraphs. The fact that a phone can be used for a business purpose would not bother us, so long as the invention also provides a technical contribution to the state-of-the-art.*

Q: The so-called 'technical effect'?

A: *We distinguish between the technical character of an invention, and the technical contribution. In talking about the 'technical effect', we mean the technical character. Now the technical character is a very weak test of patentability, as it is very easy to find a 'technical effect' in many things: the 'technical effect' of a telephone is that it transforms and transports sounds from one place to another.*

Q: But the telephone would have met both tests?

A: *Yes. The invention of the telephone also provided a technical contribution to the state-of-the-art, so it would have been regarded as patentable by the EPO.*

Q: Can you expand on the difference between technical character and 'technical effect'?

A: *A lampshade has a technical character: it is manufactured and its 'technical effect' is that it shades light. In that sense a new lampshade is not excluded from patentability. If lampshades were normally painted with pictures of roses, but somebody painted them with tulips instead we would then apply the next test, asking what contribution to the art the new lampshade made that was not already known.*

Q: And here it would fail?

A: *Right. As the change was merely aesthetic, or commercial, it would fail this test, and so would not be patentable.*

Q: This is different to the US approach?

A: *Yes. It is a critical difference. The US talks about a patent being allowable for any new and useful process, machine, manufacture, or composition of matter. That requirement more or less corresponds to our definition as to what constitutes the technical character.*

Q: The US does not look for a technical contribution?

A: *The US merely stipulates that the invention should be new and useful. We have the requirement for a technical contribution to the state-of-the-art. Therein lies the difference.*

Q: A lot of people argue that the Internet has grown so fast because it was built on open source, non-proprietary, technology. Introducing the patent system into this kind of environment, they claim, threatens that pace of development. Do you agree?

A: *I have some sympathy for the open source people, and I agree that these issues need to be discussed. However, it would be very difficult to find some kind of exception that would be appropriate.*

Q: So you don't believe that there is anything inherently different about the Internet that makes the traditional patent system inappropriate?

A: *There is one issue that comes up in terms of the web, and of computers in general, and that is the need for interoperability. I could, therefore, see the need for some provisions being neces-sary to ensure interoperability.*

Q: Might this require some restriction on what can be done with patents, or the withholding of patents in some cases?

A: *I know of no such movement to do this, but it might be the only way of dealing with the issue.*

Q: Might we, therefore, see governments concluding that the devel-opment of the Internet is so important that they need to inter-vene in the patent process?

A: *This is possible. However, in practical terms it is not very likely. If you consider America, the value of some of these patents is so high, and they belong to companies that are so valuable to US international earnings, that the US is unlikely to cut off its nose to spite its face – which is what it would be doing if it took this route.*

Q: Overall, then, you think that, like earlier new industries and technologies, the web will eventually be absorbed by the patent system?

A: *I do.*

Q: You have described the difference between the US patenting approach, and that in Europe. Is the US putting a lot of pressure on other countries to adopt their way of doing things?

A: *One has honestly to say yes to that question. The US is the most powerful single economy in the world and it is evolving more and more into an economy that relies on IP. So IP is very, very important to the Americans. As such they want to protect their income from IP, and would therefore very much like to export their model of offering very broad protection to patents.*

Q: Does this not mean, then, that Europe will inevitably end up adopting the US patenting model?

A: *That is for the politicians to decide.*

Q: What advice would you give to European politicians?

A: *I would say that if they want to apply the patentability principles of the American system it will mean changing the law in Europe.*

Q: Do you think they will?

A: *There is a general wish to harmonise patent systems globally, but there is no sign that European politicians want to achieve harmonisation by adopting the American system. Maybe the Americans will change their minds!*

Q: It is possible, however, that Europe will still allow the patenting of software?

A: *Right. But there is no will to remove the business method exception, which means there is currently no prospect of Europe granting patents for business methods in the broad way that the Americans are doing.*

Q: So internet patents will be less controversial in Europe?

A: *Right.*

Q: What are the implications of the current lack of harmony for governments, and patent offices?

A: *They will undoubtedly face a lot of pressure from the Americans. On the other hand, the Americans may feel some pressure in return. So we can expect controversy and mutual pressure for some time.*

Q: And patent offices presumably face a rising tide of business method applications?

A: *Correct, but the EPO had only around 500 applications in this field last year. That is not a very large number given that we have around 125,000 applications a year in total.*

Q: How many business method applications were there the year before that?

A: *Considerably less. Actually, it has doubled in a year or two.*

Q: And if it continued to double every few years it would become problematic?

A: *We certainly expect to see further increases, and this will put local stress on my department. We really need to grow in order to deal with these increased applications – the problem is that we just cannot find enough people who are of high enough quality for the work.*

Q: So applicants will be impacted too?

A: *It is inevitable that there will be an increase in backlogs in this area. However, I personally would prefer to have backlogs rather than grant bad patents.*

Chapter Five
"The answer to the machine is in the machine"
By Richard Poynder

Although the potential for intellectual property (IP) infringement has grown much greater with digital media, so too have the opportunities for preventing it, some argue. Computers might be part of the solution to the problem they created. In the oft-repeated phrase of Charles Clark, General Counsel at the International Publishers Copyright Council: "The answer to the machine is in the machine."

In recent years, therefore, a lot of effort and investment have gone into developing hardware and software tools designed to limit and control the ability to copy digital content. Likewise, a range of techniques and methods are being devised for identifying and deterring IP infringement on the web.

Patents and trademarks

Given the scale of the threat it faces, it is perhaps appropriate that these new tools are most suited to protecting copyright. As we shall see, some of the techniques used also have applications in protecting trademarks and brands.

However, in general there is no specific technology able to deter people from infringing patented methods or techniques, or indeed for detecting such infringements. "After all," says Chris Barlas, a senior consultant at London-based consultancy, Rightscom, "a patent is a piece of paper describing a process. The notion of being able to write a piece of software that can understand that process and then go out and find anyone else that is using the process is slightly remote."

But there are a number of web-accessible databases that patent owners can use to monitor potentially infringing patent applications by competitors. The *Derwent World Patents Index®* is one example.

Likewise, several web-based databases can help companies investigate whether anyone has registered their trademarks or brands as domain names. There are also services, such as French-based Questel.Orbit's Namewatcher.com, that can alert companies if new registrations are made that may impact or infringe their IP.

Additionally, companies like VI Net Searchers, whose headquarters are in London, provide services designed to alert owners of trademarks (or brands) to potential infringements. Net Searchers offers a 'brand patrol' service that runs automated searches over the entire web to detect any infringing activities, including searching domain name registration databases and discussion groups.

Such services will often also search competitors' meta-tags for any so-called 'diversionary' trademark infringements. Meta-tags are keywords, invisible to the end user, describing the content of a web site and designed to assist internet search engines direct users to appropriate sites. Using these meta-tags, infringers can illicitly misdirect traffic to their web site by listing a competitor's trademarks or brands.

British technology firm, Envision, has developed a search engine that uses artificial intelligence to provide a similar service. "We can, for instance, detect if a less well-known competitor has listed a client's trademarks or brands in order to draw in traffic, or whether it is illicitly claiming to be a licensed re-seller of the company concerned," says Envision MD, Ben Coppin.

Envision will also search for domain name registrations that may impact on a company's trademarks, including 'sound-alikes' and derogatory names such as companynamesucks.com.

Copyright

But most efforts today are focused on methods of protecting copyrighted material. These include developing various 'unique identifiers' for copyrighted files, as well as watermarks and 'trusted systems' (hardware and software tools designed to control access and enforce content usage rules) aimed at controlling the copying and distribution of content. These developments are increasingly referred to collectively as 'digital rights management', or DRM.

Unique identifiers: electronic licence plates

In looking to protect their IP on the web, rights owners realised there was a need for an appropriate infrastructure, both to facilitate the licensing and protection of copyright and as a way of tracking and monitoring individual files containing copyrighted material. If nothing else, once let loose on the high seas of the web, files are at risk of simply disappearing.

The first step is the creation of a universal identification scheme to allow unique identifiers to be given to all web-located content. With unique identifiers, points out Barlas "we are essentially talking about being able to audit where content is. If you think of the Internet as a giant library, what you are talking about is being able to know where your content is. After all, the point about intellectual property on the web is that it is not just about being able to protect it. Protection is a minor issue; the major issue is actually trading it." An effective inventory system is a primary step in establishing an efficient trading environment.

The Digital Object Identifier, or DOI system, is one attempt to do this. Originally created by the Association of American Publishers, this has subsequently been handed over to the International DOI Foundation

(IDF). The objective of the DOI is to provide a universal identification coding system that can operate as an 'electronic licensing plate' for digital content on the web – with a unique ID number assigned to each item of copyrighted content much like the ISBN used for books. By means of the DOI, users can quickly and easily access copyright, licensing and royalty information.

It is expected that these DOIs will eventually be assigned by authorised registration agencies. These agencies will also maintain the necessary infrastructure to ensure that, in the maelstrom of constantly changing URLs and web servers, these ID numbers always contain an accurate pointer to additional information about the content.

Another important component of such identification systems is meta-data (data about data). This, amongst other things, will allow copyrighted files to identify themselves, and the nature of their contents. As Barlas puts it: "Meta-data is the lifeblood of e-commerce. So the DOI has a mandatory meta-data set, allowing you, for instance, to declare the author and the date of publication, etc."

In a somewhat similar vein, in October 2000, the Recording Industry Association of America (RIAA) announced that it had appointed Barlas' company, Rightscom, to manage a new standardised ID system for sound recordings. This, announced Cary Sherman, senior executive for music systems at the RIAA, will provide "an effective identification system for digital files that is capable of specifying each unique sound recording, in all its forms."

This identification, reported online news service *CNET*, will use a digital equivalent of the common universal price code (UPC), or barcode, that marks virtually every physical product sold in stores. They will be used to identify precisely a given file's song and artist, and to determine how royalties from downloads should be distributed. They could also be used to delineate a track's use. So, for instance, if a listener downloads the song for a three day trial period instead of buying it outright, this information could be included in the identifying mark.

While not designed to protect music files from infringement as such, it is envisaged that this new system will determine if digital files meant to be sold are being exchanged free through services like Napster and Gnutella.

Watermarking: the indelible copyright notice

As currently envisaged, unique identifiers will not guarantee content from illicit copying, or appropriation by pirates. The emphasis is more on the facilitating of efficient trading of content rather than its protection.

Watermarking, on the other hand, lays a greater emphasis on protection. Here, inerasable markers are embedded into the digital file containing the copyrighted material – much like a conventional watermark. Unlike paper watermarks, however, digital watermarks are usually 'invisible' unless a user has the necessary software to detect and decode them. In this respect they are more like the indelible marker pens used to protect physical property.

This mark can contain actual copyright information, such as the author's name and email address, or an ID number along with an URL, fax number or some other means of accessing a database that holds the copyright information. "Watermarking doesn't stop anyone taking your content, but it does at least show you where it is meant to be," says Barlas. "So if you paid for some content it will signal that you are the licensee and that you shouldn't pass it on. It won't stop you giving it to anyone else, but it will show you as the legitimate licensee. It's a trackable honours system if you like."

As such, watermarking relies on rights owners being prepared to track down infringers and then taking the necessary legal action. Fortunately, on the web tracking is a simpler process than trying to locate the bicycle marked with your postcode in indelible ink that was stolen last week.

"If you look at the web site of the watermark company Digimarc, for example, you will see that they have a watermark crawler that can go out and look for any content that has been watermarked with Digimarc's technology," says Barlas. "So rights owners are able to track down their content and establish whether it is anywhere it should not be."

Encryption: the digital padlock

Today, however, the major focus of DRM developers is increasingly on ways of locking up copyrighted material with electronic padlocks – through the use of encryption techniques – and then only releasing it under certain conditions. These conditions are specified by supplier-defined 'usage rights', which are often outlined in inerasable electronic watermarks attached to the content, or in associated meta-data attached to the file.

The aim is to recover some of the attributes available to rights owners in the physical world that are lost when content is digitised. As Barlas puts it: "In an analogue environment content is fixed to bits of paper, or stuck on pieces of plastic, and you can't tear these two things apart. In the digital domain, however, your content becomes bits and bytes and, as such, is no longer attached to a medium, but to some sort of electronic carrier. Thus you have a sundering of the medium from the message. The principle of DRM techniques is to either stick them together again, or monitor when they are being used."

The most common technique involves enclosing content in secure electronic containers. US-based DRM developer InterTrust International uses its DigiBoxes to achieve this. The content is placed in the DigiBox, and then secured with an electronic key, before being sent across the web. Subsequently it can only be opened again when it arrives at an InterRights Point, but even then only where the user has a legitimate key. "So a consumer's PC could have an InterRights Point capable of opening a DigiBox – but it will only do so if the key in the InterRights Point and the key in the DigiBox match," explains Barlas.

Under this approach, therefore, the content will have a set of usage rules manacled to it. "What we do is to take unprotected content, and then wrap rights specified by the content owner around that content," explains Ranjit Singh, COO of US-based DRM developer, ContentGuard. "These can be time-based rights, where, for instance, the user can only access the content for 24 hours; access-based rights, where the user can only view the content, but not print it, or only print one copy; and price-based rights, where the type of access available is determined by the price paid."

Again, at the heart of many of these techniques will be meta-data. This can be used both to signal basic facts about the data, for instance, whether it is a photograph, a sound file or a text file, as well as to define the usage rules. The content will only be released when a legitimate user seeks to access it. Says Singh: "This is done by providing a unique electronic key that only allows access to the content in accordance with rights attached to it."

Other methods

DRM also encompasses a number of other methods and techniques. For instance, while primarily thought of as a way of squeezing large files more quickly across the networks, compression is an important component of DRM, since decompression can be made contingent upon the insertion of a legitimate key. After all, a file that cannot be decompressed remains unusable. "Compression technology is very, very important in DRM," says Barlas. "Compression technology and encryption go together."

Other methods currently being developed include the use of 'self-protecting document' systems, where active documents are able to preserve their integrity, and enforce rights associated with the document by a variety of means, including self-destruction. New York-based Lockstream has developed an encryption model that can degrade the image quality of eBooks – as a form of self-destruct – when illegally copied.

Additionally, DRM developers are turning their attentions to artificial intelligence. One current approach uses complex pattern recognition techniques pioneered in the human genome analysis work. "This is similar to watermarking techniques," says John Schwarz, chief executive of US DRM company, Reciprocal, "and the principle can be used for any digital content. However, rather than injecting a specific watermark into the content it records its natural patterns. So if you imagine a piece of music or video, each has a very unique pattern of bits that are put together by the original creator."

Moreover, he adds, this method offers the benefits not just of watermarking, but also the security of encryption methods, as it can prevent people from illegally copying content. "The content patterns can be stored in some kind of a central database," he explains. "Then when any transaction is initiated in which content will be distributed it will refer to that database and compare it to a library of samples of copyrighted content. If it recognises copyrighted material then it will prevent any distribution without the appropriate authority."

A maturing market

As a consequence of escalating concerns over piracy, the DRM market has now started to develop rapidly. It is also broadening its scope. While initially most DRM companies tended to focus on documents and textual data, increasingly they are looking to produce cross-media solutions. In the wake of growing concern over file swapping services like Napster and Scour, ContentGuard has begun to develop solutions for digital audio and video too.

Likewise, where the initial impetus of the DOI was to assist publishers to sell individual journal articles by means of linking citations to full-text files on the web, it is increasingly viewed as a tool for a range of other types of content as well, including audio and video. Last October, the IDF announced a new DOI-EB working group with a view to developing DOIs for electronic books.

As a further stimulus to the market, large software companies like IBM and Microsoft have also begun to turn their attentions to DRM. When Microsoft unveiled Version 7 of the Windows Media 7 in April 2000 it announced that the Windows video playback application, Windows Media Player, also included Microsoft's Windows Media Rights Manager.

The recent flurry of interest in eBooks – with text downloaded over the Internet – has further escalated interest in DRM techniques. When, in July 2000, the Microsoft Reader was launched, it contained a DRM architecture based on ContentGuard's technology.

During 2000 there was also a wave of consolidation in the industry – including Microsoft's purchase of a chunk of ContentGuard; Adobe's purchase of Glassbook; Philips investment of $60m in digital water-mark developer, Digimarc; PricewaterhouseCoopers purchase of a stake in InterTrust; and Gemstar International's acquisition of eBook companies NuvoMedia and SoftBook Press. NuvoMedia developed the Rocket eBook, and Gemstar is a US provider of electronic program-guide services, and the creator of the VCR Plus+ instant programming system for VCRs.

All the signals suggest that rights owners can expect a lot of exciting new developments in the DRM solutions space over the next few years.

No universal panacea

It would be wrong, however, to imply that DRM can deliver a universal panacea for protecting IP on the web.

Firstly, most of the tools available today are designed to protect copyright alone although, clearly, encryption can be used for protecting patented software. Watermarking and pattern recognition tools are likely to play a role in tracing trademark and brand infringement on the web.

Secondly, technology will never be an infallible solution. For this reason most DRM solutions providers argue that although technology protection systems can always be broken, they can still provide a sufficient barrier to dissuade the average consumer from infringing. As Scot Schulte, Lead Product Manager for Windows (US) puts it: "There is no foolproof system against a professional hacker with large financial resources. The intention of DRM is really to create a 'speed bump' to help honest people stay honest."

The problem, as the DeCSS case shows, is that on the web one hacker can have considerable impact, either by widely spreading the content directly, or through disseminating an anti-circumvention device online for others to use. Either way, this poses a considerable threat to content providers. Commented Allan Adler, vice president for legal and government affairs for the Association of American Publishers, to *Wired News* in September 2000: "As fast as new encryption software ... [is] ... created, someone finds a way to break it. We found a pirated copy of a Harry Potter book online in the Microsoft Reader format within a few days of the format being released."

Moreover, points out Brandy Thomas, chief executive of US-based e-business intelligence company, Cyveillance, "DRM protection, as does most protection today, tends to break down when you switch between media. In other words, someone protects their digital pictures on the net, but then someone else scans these pictures onto the net from a magazine. This is a huge problem wherever content can be copied from an analogue format, which is everything except software."

For this reason some believe that, ironically, watermarking may actually offer a better long-term solution to piracy than heavy-duty encryption techniques. As Jean-Paul Smets, French contact for the Eurolinux Alliance, comments: "None of the existing encryption tools are safe from hacking. All the hacker needs do is to create a software emulator of the hardware device intended to play, or display, the file. They can then extract the music or content without needing to use a key. If done properly, however, watermarking, can be effective. While it cannot stop anyone from accessing copyrighted files, if they then proceed to send copies around the web they can be traced back as the source of the infringement. That is a disincentive for pirates."

Obviously, this still requires that content providers are prepared to seek out infringers and go to the trouble of prosecuting them.

The standards issue

There is another challenge to be overcome if DRM is to prove successful in the long-term. Consumers want to be able to use their content utilising any access device, or software tool, regardless of which DRM system the content is protected with. "Interoperability is absolutely key," says Barlas. "Rights owners don't want to be stuck with legacy systems, and consumers don't want to have multiple black boxes for accessing content."

Today, however, there is no agreement on standards. "Without a common language interoperability cannot happen," acknowledges Singh. "But then it depends on implementation. We are pushing for common implementations and common formats, but we are not there yet."

To encourage standardisation, ContentGuard has proposed its solution – dubbed eXtensible rights Markup Language (XrML) – as a standard. "XrML is a language that specifies how the usage rights are wrapped up," says Singh. "In order to speed up adoption rates, we have said that we will license XrML to anyone in the industry on a royalty-free basis. The aim is to provide a common language that content owners can use to specify these rights."

The problem, of course, is that other DRM players are reluctant to adopt a standard being pushed by a competitor, especially where that company is part owned by Microsoft. Andrew Robbins, commercial development manager for InterTrust, is concerned by the implications of one company dominating a standard. Moreover, InterTrust has developed its own meta-data language that is being widely adopted by content providers, as well as major infrastructure players like AOL. "AOL V 6.0 will contain InterTrust's DRM technology, which means that all content, whether it be books, music or video, that is traded over AOL in the future will be done using InterTrust's technology," says Robbins. "When it is released, AOL V 6.0 will go to all its subscribers. We have also just signed up Blockbuster, which will use our technology for its new video-on-demand service in the US."

Industry-wide approach needed

Conscious that an industry-wide approach is needed, in 1998 all the major players in the music industry, along with consumer electronics companies, DRM companies and ISPs, created the Secure Digital Music Initiative (SDMI). Today its membership numbers around 200 companies and organisations. SDMI's aim is to develop a standard that will be built into music playback devices and computer software to exploit DRM techniques.

In July 1999, version 1.0 of its Portable Device Phase I standard was issued. With Phase II - which was due to be completed by April 2000 but at the time of writing was still not finalised - it hopes to create a more elaborate protection system. The long-term aim is that all devices capable of playing music will eventually be SDMI-compliant and all songs recorded will be encrypted and embedded with a watermark that will govern how a song may be copied and played, along with details on who has to pay for it, and when.

But the example of the encryption system developed for the DVD is not encouraging. Despite cross-industry support for the CSS encryption system, a utility capable of circumventing it – DeCSS – was soon circulating on the Internet. Despite the Motion Picture Association of America's (MPAA) success in obtaining an injunction to stop the online hacker magazine, *2600*, from linking to it, DeCSS remains widely available on the web.

Whether the SDMI will prove more successful only time will tell. At the time of writing the organisation had challenged the hacker community to break into the six competing technologies being considered for Phase II, offering a $10,000 reward for anyone who successfully did so. After around 450 attempts it was widely rumoured that all systems had been broken – even though many in the hacking community had refused to take part on the grounds that it would be politically incorrect to help the enemy! However, the SDMI claimed that only two of the technologies had been broken.

After the horse has bolted?

There are also some who question whether standards-bodies like the SDMI will be able to reach agreement in time. The SDMI project is already running behind schedule. Yet the executive director of the SDMI, Dr. Leonardo Chiariglione, seemed strangely sanguine about timing when interviewed [see page 140], merely pointing out that: "It took eight years for the MP3 standard to move from the technology specification stage to widespread use."

With new-style 'peer-to-peer' (P2P) services like Freenet and Gnutella proliferating on the web, the music industry may find that, quite apart from reliability issues, it cannot move fast enough. There are also approximately ten billion unprotected music CDs already out there, and some suggest that the approach of the SDMI smacks of trying to shut the stable door after the horse has bolted. "The RIAA initially allowed people to copy and distribute music files – now they're trying to implement DRM, and it's too late as the precedent has been set," argues Thomas.

A right too far?

But if initiatives like SDMI do prove successful they will exacerbate the growing concern that DRM techniques threaten the traditional 'bargain' between IP owners and society.

This argument says that while DRM techniques may be susceptible to the determined hacker, they interpose an unacceptable barrier to members of the public wanting to exercise their 'fair use' rights. While it is simple for a user to copy a page of a book with a photocopier, or record an episode of NYPD on a video recorder (both legitimate activities under current copyright laws), the barriers imposed by DRM technologies remove this right from all but the skilled technologist.

The fact that DRM technologies are expected, in the future, to be built into the hardware of all PCs and consumer devices only aggravates these concerns. "In the future, DRM will be part of every digital environment," explained Talal Shamoon vice president of media at DRM company, InterTrust, to *InfoWorld* in June 2000. "It will be part of the OS [operating system], part of the portable devices, part of the server – it will be part of the computer."

It is also expected that initiatives, like that of the SDMI, will eventually see all content encrypted from the moment it is created. "The new standards coming down the technology pipeline will encrypt the media before it is ever available to the public," says Schwarz. "So eventually even the free music will go away, as it will never be available in unencrypted format."

The concern here is that while rights owners will be able to 'lock up' their content using DRM technology, and then release it only in accordance with their own rules, users will be disenfranchised. No longer will they be able to make copies for their personal use for instance. As Wendy Seltzer, Fellow of the Berkman Centre for Internet & Society, Harvard Law School, puts it [see page 145]: "While it's true that digital media take away control that rights owners had, I worry that they are overcompensating and putting in technological measures that enhance their control to the public detriment. I am also concerned that technological measures – or code – cannot balance issues of 'fair use' as a court must."

DRM developers dispute this: "There is nothing that technology does that makes the problem of 'fair use' any different to what it is today with physical formats," says Schwarz. "In fact, if anything media owners have the ability to provide access in a far more flexible, user-friendly and innovative way."

Moreover, he argues, DRM allows content providers to offer users a far broader selection of content than previously. "The major music companies will have anything between 30,000 and 50,000 titles in their inventory. But, at any one point, probably less than 10% of that is available on CDs in their stores."

With new laws like the Digital Millennium Copyright Act (DMCA) and the proposed EU Copyright Directive outlawing actions to 'reverse engineer' digital encryption systems, the 'fair use' lobby is becoming increasingly vocal. Opponents are concerned that new legislation is also making it illegal for technologists to help the unskilled consumer exercise 'fair use' rights. They also argue that the law is impacting on other civil rights, as well as raising anti-trust, issues. Questions like this have already been raised in the DeCSS case, with critics arguing that the DMCA has outlawed attempts by open source programmers to develop a DVD player for the Linux operating system.

Contract law to supplant copyright?

Additionally, there is increasing concern that DRM is allowing rights owners to supplant IP laws with contract law, which further erodes the balance between the rights of IP owners and those of users.

In particular, there are concerns that DRM techniques will foist usage rules on users by means of 'click-through' licences that the user does not understand the significance of. "Under copyright law you have the right to 'fair use' of a movie, for example," says Seltzer. "If you had to click through a licence before you watched a movie for the first time they could now say: 'forget copyright law; as a matter of contract you are prevented from doing anything more than we permit.' I can see the same thing happening to music."

Another worrying development, she adds, is the introduction of new 'features' that enforce unpublicised usage rules. "DRM can impose limits that the user purchasing a disc has no idea exist," she explains. "Currently I think this is only being used to prevent things like the fast forwarding of the commercials that appear at the beginning of DVD movies – but many people purchase these discs without knowing that it includes this so-called feature."

However, while this is worrying for lawyers and civil libertarians, DRM developers are inclined to view this 'transparency' as a plus. "Windows Media Rights Manager was designed to allow content providers to hide the DRM technology behind their own retail experience," says Schulte. "The encrypted content can be played on most media players and the licence acquisition is virtually transparent, so the user can quickly acquire the content and easily play it."

Striking a balance

It cannot be doubted that DRM has an important role to play for content providers. But as we have seen, there are dangers – not least of being seen to remove user rights in the process of protection.

In fact, suggests Lawrence Lessig, in his book *Code and Other Laws of Cyberspace*, the power of technology means that rights owners now need to focus less on protection, and more on their responsibilities to the public. The real question, he says "is not, how can law aid in …[the protection of IP] … but rather, is the protection too great."

Lessig adds: "The lesson in the future will be that copyright is protected far too well. The problem will centre not on 'copy-right' but on 'copy-duty' – the duty of owners of protected property to make that property accessible."

Finally, DRM also raises usability issues. "If, in order to listen to a two-second tune, consumers have to enter 58 different numbers, give six separate passwords, and then put their fingerprint on a smart card, they are simply not going to bother," points out Barlas facetiously.

When, in 2000, Universal Music Group launched its new bluematter technology– designed to allow users to download single music tracks over the web – it attracted just such criticism. Even before the launch it was being widely slated for being unwieldy and expensive. In September 2000, Bob Kohn, chief executive of web music site, EMusic.com, was quoted in *PC World* as saying that the file encryption system used in bluematter posed a significant barrier to usage. It was, he said, "very un-user friendly. It is embarrassing." Anyone who has tried to buy music using bluematter technology will endorse these concerns.

In looking to exploit DRM solutions, content providers are clearly going to have to strike a delicate balance. If the measures they adopt are too easily circumvented, their content will not be adequately protected. And if the measures prove too onerous, or too cumbersome, for consumers to use comfortably, the content will not be accessed. However, if the measures are transparent, yet impose licensing terms that users are not aware are being used (or are subsequently perceived as being unfair), rights owners may again alienate their customers – a particularly dangerous issue on the web, where there is a culture and practice of freely available content.

For these reasons some are sceptical that DRM is an appropriate solution. Thomas concludes: "In the long-term, there is very little you can do to protect your IP. In the short-term, you can only make it more difficult for people to copy and identify who's copying it. ... [so] ... the fundamental question a company must consider is whether they ought to be trying to protect their IP, or whether they ought to be exploiting the misuse of their IP to benefit them, and add new revenue streams."

Richard Poynder interviews Dr Leonardo Chiariglione, Executive Director, the Secure Digital Music Initiative (SDMI)

Q: What is the purpose of SDMI?

A: *The aim is to define the framework that will allow e-commerce in digital music to take place in a protected format.*

Q: And this will be done by developing new technology standards for playing music on portable devices and PCs. Where have you got with this?

A: *The first phase was to define the features and characteristics of this framework, and the portable device specification 1.0 was approved in June 1999. The second phase is to develop technologies to allow a device to recognise whether a music file submitted for playback is an old music file - in the sense that it is has been ripped from one of the ten billion compact discs that have been published in the last seventeen years - or whether it is new music published under the SDMI regime.*

Q: How many members of SDMI are there?

A: *Around two hundred.*

Q: Music companies and consumer electronics and PC manufacturers?

A: *Virtually everybody with a stake in digital music is a member.*

Q: How will SDMI technology work?

A: *We do not plan to define the specifics of the technology, only the security levels. The intention is to standardise the environment in order to enable interoperability, not to standardise around a single protection technology.*

Q: Presumably these standards will be based on Digital Rights Management (DRM) techniques – using encrypted music files only capable of being decrypted using a valid electronic key purchased by the user?

A: *Absolutely.*

Q: So encryption is central. What about watermarking?

A: *Watermarking will be used to signal whether the music is old or new; and where it is detected to be new, whether it has been pirated or not.*

Q: You say SDMI technology will differentiate between old and new music. Presumably the new devices will still play old music – such as CD music or MP3 files?

A: *SDMI-compliant devices will play legacy content without restriction.*

Q: In the future, then, people will use special players – or they will play music on their PC that has been downloaded from the Internet – and this music will be encrypted. Additionally, it will contain rules restricting the way in which it can be used.

A: *Exactly: these are the 'usage' rules.*

Q: Critics argue that this approach will restrict consumers' legal rights to copy content for private use under the 'fair usage' principle.

A: *In an analogue environment illegal copying is not always a simple process, but to prevent people from doing it would require assigning a policeman to every single member of the population. In the digital domain, any piece of content can be copied and distributed to ten million people with a stroke of a key, but content owners now have access to powerful technologies for protecting that content. I do not say this is right or wrong. There may well be claims that consumers are put at a disadvantage as a result.*

Q: You blame the technology, not the content owners?

A: *No. My point is simply that to have content retain its value in the digital domain you must protect it. If it is not protected, content has no value. I would add that usage rules also offer advantages to consumers.*

Q: What kind of advantages?

A: *When you buy a CD today, and it is yours for ever – whether you listen to it once or whether you listen to it 24 hours a day – you always pay the same price. Usage rules offer more flexibility. You could be offered a discount if you buy a song that can only be played for a limited number of times.*

Q: Critics like the Electronic Frontier Foundation (EFF) argue that SDMI is only concerned about the rights of content owners, not about the rights of consumers, and that it is not a very open process. How do you respond to that criticism?

A: *SDMI is an open body and if you want to join you send a letter and apply. I see all the application forms myself and I can tell you that anybody can join. Did you know that Napster is a member of SDMI? If the EFF wants to be an advocate of consumer interests in this matter then they would be better arguing their case within SDMI, not outside it.*

Q: It is widely held that all security technology can be hacked into. How confident are you that SDMI-compliant encryption and watermarking techniques will prove effective?

A: *If we had adopted the approach of standardising on a single protection scheme, such concerns might be real. But that is not what SDMI is doing. We are defining security levels, not the security technology itself. There won't be a single protection scheme.*

Q: But if all protection technology can be disabled, music companies wanting to protect their copyright on the web remain at risk of piracy?

A: *The aim is not to develop a standard for security but the APIs [Application Programming Interfaces] through which a protection algorithm can be downloaded and run on a machine to decode the content. Theoretically every single piece of content could be encrypted using a different algorithm, so every time you buy a piece of content you buy with that content the usage rules, as well as the protection scheme needed to run on your device to decrypt the content. While it is true that a hacker could crack the protection of one specific song, the breach would be limited to that song alone, and every song would have to be cracked from scratch.*

Q: You say that approximately ten billion CDs have been sold over the last seventeen years. Given this, is not the SDMI initiative akin to shutting the stable door after the horse has bolted? None of those ten billion CDs is currently protected.

A: *It's true that a recording of an opera made ten years ago is as valuable as that same opera published today, but for a much larger portion of the music market the past is the past. What matters most is the new music being published.*

Q: What are your timelines for wide scale use of SDMI-compliant music?

A: *I could give you SDMI's timeline for issuing the specifications. But then you would have to factor in the timeline needed for manufacturers to make SDMI-compliant products. Then you have a third timeline: the time it takes for the bulk of consumers to adopt those products. You will understand that these last two are out of SDMI's control.*

Q: What are your ambitions?

A: *We have ambitions, but we have to be realistic. It is one thing to have a technology ready: quite another for that technology to become the dominant technology in the marketplace. The MP3 standard was approved in November 1992. It has taken around eight years for that technology to become the mass phenomenon it is today.*

Q: If it took another eight years to see SDMI-compliant music become a mass phenomenon there would surely be little hope of stopping the threat of file-swapping services like Napster and Gnutella?

A: *You always have to work for something, rather than against it. Let me say how this basic principle can be applied in the Napster case. A simple definition of Napster is that it is the best possible distribution means ever invented by human beings. The only problem is that because most content today is unprotected it leads to mass piracy abuses. Imagine that instead of content being released in unprotected form it was released in protected form. Napster would then become a great tool for content owners – because it would allow them to distribute their content in a way never before seen in the history of mankind.*

Q: So Napster will turn out to be a good thing for the industry?

A: *Eventually. After all, the Internet was the terror of telecom companies five years ago. Today it has become a very, very substantial source of revenue – because people are using their phone lines so much more.*

Richard Poynder interviews Wendy Seltzer, Fellow of the Berkman Centre for Internet & Society, Harvard Law School

Q: You are a Fellow at the Harvard Berkman Centre and you lead the Openlaw project. What is Openlaw?

A: *Openlaw is an effort to bring the methods of open source software development to legal argument in the public interest. On copyright issues, we try to give a voice to the public domain. As new laws like the US Digital Millennium Copyright Act (DMCA) impact the public's rights to use new digital media and the Internet, Openlaw aims to provide a forum for members of the public to respond.*

Q: What are your primary concerns about the use of DRM technologies?

A: *My chief concern is that technological protections can give copyright owners much more absolute control over their works than they ever had in the pre-digital environment. While it's true that digital media take away the control that rights owners had, I worry that they are over-compensating and putting in technological measures that enhance their control to the public detriment. I am also concerned that technological measures - or code - cannot balance issues of 'fair use' as a court must.*

Q: Rights owners usually respond by arguing that DRM actually gives them greater control to allow 'fair use'?

A: *But they allow 'fair use' only in a circumscribed way. They may, for instance, allow you to lend an e-Book twice, but not three times; or to print one page, but not 10. In the US at least, the courts have always said that 'fair use' must be analysed on a case-by-case basis. What is unfair use in one context may be fair in another. Different uses are appropriate for a teacher's classroom presentation, a critic's demonstration, and an artist's reference to predecessor works. With DRM, a lot of uses that may be fair are blocked by technology that treats everyone the same, no matter what they are trying to do.*

Q: You have also been involved with the DeCSS case - in which [studio members of the] MPAA sued a web site for facilitating the trafficking of a software utility [DeCSS] designed to disable the encryption system used on DVDs. What was your role there?

A: *I helped draft an amicus [neutral friend of court] brief that Openlaw participants filed with the district court. We wanted to draw attention to the free speech issues raised by prohibiting the trafficking of circumvention technology. We also argued that in hearing such cases, the courts should take into account the important role that reverse engineering [establishing, for example, how an encryption system works by de-compiling it] plays in enabling people to learn about technology.*

Q: In the event, the judge ruled in favour of the MPAA. Why was this case considered by the courts before the US Copyright Office had defined the exemptions under which circumventing techno-logical protection measures was permitted?

A: *Well, the DeCSS case is being appealed. But there are two distinct prohibitions: on use of circumvention devices and on their distribution. The Copyright Office can specify classes of works for which the use of circumvention devices is permitted, but even those exemptions won't apply to the trafficking of circumvention devices at issue in the DeCSS case. For the exempt classes of works, the DMCA essentially says that if you can figure out how to bypass technological measures on your own, you are free to do so without prosecution, but if you can't do it yourself, you are stuck.*

Q: So in the US it is legal for individuals in certain circumstances to bypass DRM technology, but always illegal to share circumvention devices, or even to tell others how to circumvent?

A: *That's the way it looks. If you're part of the great mass of users who don't understand the technology, these exemptions are of no use to you.*

Q: Where does the discussion about Napster fit in here? There has been a lot of heat generated by the case, but initiatives like the SDMI are focused on encrypting all music before it leaves the recording studio. This suggests that music swapping will become pointless in the future, given that anyone downloading music files won't be able to listen to them without buying a key?

A: *Meanwhile there are hundreds of thousands of unencrypted CDs out there, and nothing is going to take them out of circulation. Besides, all these encryption schemes are somewhat utopian. Eventually all music files have to be decrypted to play. At that point, people can record the unencrypted copy. They may not be able to do this using SDMI-compliant recording devices, but they will be able to use other devices that have those capabilities.*

Q: So once it is decrypted it will be possible to hijack the signal and record it in an unencrypted form?

A: *Right. If there is any place that people can put software into the process, or take an output from somewhere else in the playback mechanism, there is room to record.*

Q: So DRM technology is not going to be particularly effective anyway?

A: *Not against everyone, unless there is very intrusive legislation, essentially surveillance of what people are doing with their technology.*

Q: Many DRM developers point out that their only aim is to act as a 'speed bump', not to produce totally impregnable barriers?

A: *And the aim of the DMCA is to 'keep honest people honest'! This is an elitist view: it says that those who have the skills to get around protections that violate their rights can do so, while those who don't are stuck with the more limited playback capacities of the new players that will be introduced. Besides, if there is legislation backing these devices, and yet even the implementers think of them only as speed bumps, then we are creating laws that we expect to be broken. That doesn't foster much respect for law.*

Q: What's your response to content owners who say they need to make a living and cannot produce content if people take it without paying?

A: *Copyright is not an absolute right. It is not a property like physical property and copyright laws don't protect the rights owners in their choice of business model. If their distribution model isn't working, then they should be looking for other ways of distributing content, not locking down content distributed under old models.*

Q: There have been a number of internet copyright cases. Are the courts not doing enough to protect consumer rights?

A: *To date the rulings have been very deferential to the rights owners and this is worrying. I have to hope that the higher courts will re-think the issues and conclude that it was not intended that IP should be protected in such an absolutist manner. As the measures become more invasive, it may be easier to make the argument that Congress did not intend this outcome or, if intended, that it does not comport with constitutional restrictions.*

Q: Do you expect politicians to get involved in the debate?

A: *I think Congress will be asked to look at this again, if only because services like Napster have managed to stir enough public concern. I'm not yet confident they'll strike the right balance between public rights and private control.*

Q: Given the global nature of the web, this debate reaches beyond the US. Suppose the EU takes a more consumer-oriented approach to the use of DRM and circumvention devices: what might be the implications?

A: *We could end up with an enclave of protected reverse engineers in Europe, while those in the US were prohibited from trafficking in the devices, and perhaps prohibited from even using them. Such inconsistencies could be another force against hyper-protectionism.*

Q: What are your main concerns about DRM?

A: *My biggest concern is that all of these so-called 'trusted systems' are based on a basic distrust of the user. They make any curiosity or investigation about the technology illegal. Moreover, the degree to which they can limit our access to copyrighted works means that these works cease being cultural fixtures and become private individual publications, a process some refer to as 'privacation'.*

Q: What advice would you give to rights owners?

A: *They should respect the public, and their curiosity and desire to learn about technology, by allowing them to use technology freely. They should also look for new business models based on partnerships with the public rather than trying to wall-off content from them.*

Q: And your advice to governments?

A: *Governments should be ready to give some oversight to the codes that will control the use of IP. They should recognise that rights owners can claim far more power with these technological measures than they otherwise had and should make sure the public is still getting its fair share of the bargain.*

Q: What will happen in the longer term?

A: *People will start to understand the limitations DRM imposes and the rights that they are giving up. At that point DRMs will either adapt and become more permissive, or they will be regulated. We are not going to eliminate DRM technology: it is too powerful to just disappear. So the right approach is to understand that it is a new form of control, a new form of regulation, and that limits need to be set on how it is used.*

Chapter Six
Assume the rules may change
By Richard Poynder

The web, then, is having a significant impact on traditional intellectual property (IP), making it both far more valuable and yet far more vulnerable. It is also introducing many new uncertainties.

But is traditional IP irrelevant in the age of the web, or are we simply going through a period of transition? Right now, we simply don't know.

As we have seen, traditionalists refute suggestions that the web destroys the *raison d'être* of IP. To support their case they point out that previous attempts at jettisoning traditional IP have always failed. When the French abolished copyright, in 1789, all its creative writers left the country in order to publish elsewhere, says Rightscom's Barlas. "All that got published was pornographic material and seditious pamphlets. As a result France re-introduced copyright in 1793."

Likewise, those who support the status quo argue that, when the Netherlands abolished the patent system at the end of the 19th Century, companies simply filed their patents abroad. Twenty years later, worried about the impact the decision was having on the Dutch economy, Holland re-introduced patents.

Forget history, insist the radicals, the Internet is so dramatically different to anything that has gone before that – like it or not – we are going to have to accept that traditional IP does not work in a web economy. "The war is on, all right, but to my mind it's over," said the vice chairman of the Electronic Frontier Foundation, John Perry Barlow, in *Wired* magazine in October 2000. "The future will win; there will be no property in cyberspace."

The corporate perspective

The key issue for owners of IP right now is deciding whether, in migrating their businesses to the web, they should continue to rely on traditional IP laws to protect them, or whether they should assume that, when entering cyberspace, they must leave behind many of the rules and certainties operating in the physical world.

For copyright owners, the first question is whether to make their content available on the web at all. Many publishers have taken the plunge, but few are yet making money from these activities. At the same time a good many others – including the publishers of well-known print magazines like *The New Yorker* and *Vanity Fair* – continue to refrain from publishing on the web.

But the problem is more subtle than simply deciding whether to 'play' on the web. While music companies have been hugely reluctant to make their content available online, P2P services like Napster have demonstrated that this is no guarantee of safety, as consumers are distributing music on the web for them. So, even where rights owners have withheld their content from the Internet, it is nevertheless leaking online – and at a very rapid pace.

This is a harsh truth that the film, software and book publishing industries are becoming increasingly aware of too. In September 2000, for instance, *Wired News* reported that dozens of best-selling novels by authors such as Stephen King and J K Rowling were available for download at a site called #Bookwarez, although the site disappeared after the story was published.

These sites, commented internet consultant R H Dale to *Wired News*, "simply operate until they get caught, close down, and re-appear under a new name within 24 hours."

Protecting trademarks (and brands) on the web is problematic for all companies. While the efforts of the Internet Corporation for Assigned Names and Numbers (ICANN) and the World Intellectual Property Organisation (WIPO) to introduce some certainties offer hope, current plans to introduce a whole raft of new top level domains will surely only escalate concerns about cyber-squatting.

Moreover, following its first open elections in October 2000, the ICANN board saw a number of new members elected, including two who are openly critical of the organisation, alleging that it is biased towards business interests. This could herald new challenges for rights owners. One of the new members, Andy Mueller-Maguhn, a German programmer, stated to *Wired News* that his election demonstrated that "the type of big-business lobbyists who have dominated ICANN .... were unable to muster serious support."

An IP arms race

In addition, IP rights cut both ways. Rights owners may themselves be confronted with escalating demands for royalties on hundreds of basic web-based business processes. Those possessing such patents, on the other hand, may experience increasing problems enforcing them in the face of intense criticism from the web community.

Given the current environment, businesses today are engaged in an IP arms race, acquiring as many domain names and web-based patents as possible in order to ward off competitors. They are also becoming increasingly aggressive in protecting their copyright on the Internet.

Many companies, for instance, are creating large arsenals of patents, to be used when confronted with licensing demands from competitors.

As Gordon Petrash points out [see page 23], we now live in an environment in which it is better to have patents that might eventually be disallowed, than to be left fighting weaponless with those who do have them.

The downside is that companies could wind up devoting most of their time and money to legal disputes over IP, rather than building good businesses. If one considers that it costs around $1m today for each side to 'slug out' even a relatively simple patent dispute, this is surely not a desirable outcome.

An absurd situation

The current obsession with acquiring more and more IP is becoming a source of unease for many companies, and for some lawyers too. Fear of the anti-competitive consequences of business method patents is a particular concern. "I cannot see much inventive activity in developing a method for ordering products over the Internet that can be executed with a single mouse click [the '1-Click' patent issued to Amazon.com]," comments Viktor Rainer, an IP lawyer at Munich-based IP firm Vossius & Partner. "An absurd situation would arise if all orders or transactions via the Internet can only be performed by several mouse clicks, except at Amazon.com, which has a monopoly thereon."

Domain name registrations that appear to bias certain sections of the business community are another contentious issue. "One could have the impression that large corporations enjoy privileges which are not easily justified," says Dr. Thure Schubert, a partner at Vossius & Partner. "In view of their need for worldwide representation, large corporations are sometimes granted domain names even if another person has the same name, and was the first to reserve the domain name."

When EMI Music Publishing filed a copyright suit against a Santa Monica start-up called YourMobile.com in August 2000, many felt that an element of the absurd was also invading the arena of copyright.

EMI's complaint was that YourMobile.com was using the Internet to help people change the ring of their mobile phones into beeping melodies of popular tunes owned by EMI, including John Lennon's 'Imagine' and the Rolling Stones' 'Start Me Up'. EMI demanded up to $45m in damages for this. Commenting on the suit, an anonymous analyst joked to the *Los Angeles Times* that soon the music industry was liable to go after people who sing in their shower. In the current environment, some fear that the joke may prefigure reality.

The consumer's perspective?

We saw in chapter five how rights owners are also resorting to ever more sophisticated electronic tools for 'locking up' IP on the web, which raises some disquiet about the possible impact this could have on consumer rights. Consumer groups are also concerned about the potential impact on consumer rights of the continual extension of IP laws, and the consequent 'propertisation' of knowledge.

Once again, lawyers are worried also. "An increased 'propertisation' of knowledge involves the risk that the balance between individual rights and general interest will be upset," says Dr. Schubert. "If the underlying rationale of IP rights is to spur research and development by granting the inventor a reward for his efforts, then the crucial questions are the following. Which inventions (in the broadest sense) are worth a reward and what reward may reasonably be expected?"

Reminding us that IP was always meant to be a 'bargain' between rights owners and society, critics argue that the ongoing strengthening of IP is disrupting the balance assumed in that bargain. For instance, they argue, by enacting new legislation such as the Sono Bono Copyright Term Extension Act (extending copyright protection by 20 years), the US government is tilting the balance away from the public interest.

And when laws and technology become too onerous, they add, the system begins to fall over. In his book *Code and Other Laws of Cyberspace*, Professor Lessig points out that there are four basic ways for society to regulate the behaviour of its members: through the law, through social norms, through market forces (essentially pricing) and through architecture (technological constraints). He adds that if the laws become too draconian, then people are inclined to simply ignore them, for example as many currently do with speed limits.

The Napster phenomenon, argued John Perry Barlow, in *Wired* magazine in October 2000, demonstrates this clearly. "No law can be successfully imposed on a huge population that does not morally support it and possesses easy means for its invisible evasion."

The limits of the law

In so far as they define the legal infrastructure, governments clearly have a very important role to play in this debate. The Digital Millennium Copyright Act (DMCA), the Sono Bono Copyright Term Extension Act, the EU E-commerce and Copyright Directives, the Anti-Cyber-squatting Consumer Protection Act, along with ICANN's Uniform Domain Name Dispute Resolution Policy (UDRP), all reflect governmental determination to provide IP with comparable protection in cyberspace as is available in the physical world. With this same aim in mind, the US courts have gradually extended the scope of patentability to encompass both software and, more recently, business methods.

But this approach is not without its problems. As we have seen, it has raised public interest questions. It is also proving increasingly difficult for laws to keep pace with technology – a point conceded by Marybeth Peters, head of the US Copyright office, when interviewed by *Warren's Washington Internet Daily* in September 2000.

Ms. Peters pointed out that the entire basis of internet copyright regulation may have to be reviewed if Napster, or a similar firm, wins in court. Companies such as Napster, she said, were "not part of the calibration" in the Capitol Hill negotiations that led to the DMCA. "We weren't that visionary," she said.

The perspective of government

Governments also face a conflict of interest. In their determination to benefit from the 'first-mover advantage' of re-engineering their national economies for the web, they are beginning to suspect that 'propping up' old economy companies' traditional business methods could end up handicapping the best and the brightest of the new economy entrepreneurs.

Amongst other things this is causing tension between different government departments. Amidst the pile of 'friends-of-court' briefs filed in connection with the Recording Industry Association of America's (RIAA) court application to shut down Napster were statements from the US Justice Department and the US Copyright Office. They both argued that if Napster was allowed to exist in its current form its "users would be permitted to engage in digital copying and public distribution of copyright works on a scale beggaring anything Congress could have imagined when it enacted the DMCA. Yet the music industry would receive nothing in return."

Stung into a response, Orrin Hatch, chairman of the powerful Senate Judiciary Committee, immediately wrote to the Court to point out that this did not represent the opinion of all the US government. "Given the importance of the issues to be decided," he said, "I thought it important that the court be under no misapprehension that the (DOJ) brief necessarily expresses the view of Congress in this matter."

Tellingly, at an earlier meeting of the Senate Judiciary Committee, Senator Hatch had commented. "We must protect the rights of the creator. But we cannot, in the name of copyright, unduly burden consumers and the promising technology the Internet presents to all of us."

At a crossroads

National governments are currently at a crossroads. One route is to continue passing, and encouraging proactive enforcement of, new IP laws. The other is to take a step back to re-assess the situation.

As in the US, the initial response of European politicians has been hard-line – with the e-commerce and copyright directives conceived as European equivalents to the DMCA. Following growing evidence that the infringing activities enabled by services like Napster may evade the law, some European politicians are proposing even more interventionist approaches. In August 2000, for instance, the German Justice Minister, Herta Däubler-Gmelin, called for an IP fee to be imposed on computer equipment, thereby creating funds that would allow annual payments to musicians, artists and writers.

Subsequently supported by Chancellor Gerhard Schroeder, this new 'tax' could eventually be applied to devices like CD burners, disk drives and high-speed modems used to reproduce or download copyrighted works. But the German electronics industry is up in arms over the proposal, arguing that the fees are unfair and will lead to a decline in use of the Internet in Germany.

Europe, like the US, has also taken a hard-line approach to cybersquatting. Some politicians have been sympathetic to calls for European patent laws to be extended in line with those of the US because of concern that European companies could be placed at a competitive disadvantage due to the greater ease with which US companies can obtain patents on software and business methods.

Second thoughts?

More recently, however, questions have begun to be asked about the potential risks and costs of a too enthusiastic enforcement of IP rights on the Internet, particularly if it were to dampen down the development of the web.

Again, the debate has to date been most evident in the US. Sparked by concern that the RIAA's legal actions against new-style music companies such as MP3.com are in danger of harming the development of the internet economy, US Democrat Representative, Rick Boucher, introduced in the House of Representatives in September 2000 a bill called the Music Owners' Listening Rights Act.

If successful, the new bill would amend copyright law to legitimatise music 'locker' services like My.MP3.com – for which MP3.com was earlier in the year successfully sued by the Motion Picture Association of America (MPAA). "What matters is whether new technologies are consistent with the theory of the copyright laws, not just consistent with the details of the copyright law," Boucher told *The New York Times*. "The law should not stand in the way of an entirely legitimate technology that provides consumer convenience without costing the record companies anything." While this would be too late to save MP3.com the massive damages it was ordered to pay for copyright violations, it is a clear signal that US politicians are beginning to worry about the consequences of over-draconian IP laws.

Commenting on the bill, *The New York Times* said: "At a time when technology is evolving so rapidly and the stakes are so high over who can exercise how much control over copyrighted works, there may be cause for Congress to look more closely at the rights it has doled out in the past, and how those rights are being applied now."

Patents too

A month later Boucher, along with fellow Democrat congressman Howard Berman, introduced the Business Method Patent Improvement Act of 2000, aimed at amending application procedures for business method patents by adding "new protections to the beginning and end of the current process ... [allowing the public to submit] ... evidence that the claimed invention is already in use."

"This bill came from a shared concern about the way business method patents are awarded. It's time to inject some healthy scepticism back into the process," said Boucher. Amongst other things the bill would establish an 'opposition procedure' at the conclusion of the process "so that the public at large would have one additional opportunity to challenge the award of a business method patent short of having to file a lawsuit," Boucher explained.

Even if it succeeded, however, the bill would still leave the US some way ahead of both Europe and Japan in terms of the breadth of patentability available for US companies looking to patent e-commerce methods.

Meanwhile in Europe....

Meanwhile, in Europe, the debate on software and business method patenting looks set to become as controversial as in the US. As we saw in chapter four, on 19th October 2000 the European Commission launched consultations on the patentability of computer-implemented inventions, to be completed by December 15th. "There is a passionate debate raging on both sides," chief executive of the UK Patent Office, Alison Brimelow, told the *Financial Times*. "The Commission recognises that any policy move is likely to prove controversial, but believes it has to address the issue."

As a result of the EC decision, delegates to the Munich EPC Diplomatic Conference, who had planned to make changes to Article 52 of the EPC, for example to remove the current European exclusion of software from patentability, suddenly found their hands tied. "The action of the EC stayed the hand of the EPC, which had planned to remove the current ban on the patenting of software, and extended the consultation process," says Bob Hart, chairman of the Computer Technology Committee of the UK's Chartered Institute of Patent Agents (CIPA). "What appears to have happened is that the EC was flooded with objections from the European open source movement, which is opposed to the patenting of software."

Time will tell how this theme plays out. What seems clear, however, is that governments now realise that the electorate is getting restive. As *The New York Times* put it in reporting on the Music Owners' Listening Rights Act bill. "This bill is significant because, for the first time in this year's digital music wars, it raises the question of what is right, rather than what is legal."

Nationalisation of IP?

Spurred on by concerns over the patenting of genes, some commentators even go so far as to propose that certain types of IP will be nationalised. Rather than aiding the ongoing privatisation of knowledge, they argue, a government's role should be to begin rolling back the process, and restoring the balance in favour of society at large. Here we can see the debate over the future of IP on the web paralleling discussions over the patenting of genes – in which some commentators have argued for the public ownership of IP.

Seth Shulman [see page 27], for instance, is a staunch opponent of the trend of patenting methods of doing business. "What we are finding, again and again, is that to allow a private entity to own a key piece of the infostructure [the whole information infrastructure that supports and facilitates the web] causes a lot of problems," he says. Consequently, he concludes, the priority for governments now is "to amend the rules to protect our collective vision of the infostructure from the worst excesses of private exploitation."

Today, he adds, governments are mistakenly leaving it to the courts, or market forces, to resolve the issues. "The problem is that we are viewing it in a very legalistic way, or in a very limited economic way," he says. "In fact, these issues are a matter of public policy."

While nationalisation today may seem a highly improbable scenario, it does seem likely that there will be a new focus on the social consequences of IP in future discussion about IP and the web.

Relinquishing control

Whatever governments do, the current ethos of the web poses significant market challenges for rights owners. After all, the web ethos assumes that all content should be free, and all development undertaken collaboratively and in non-proprietary mode. In such an environment how can IP prevail? How can it win hearts and minds?

One issue is that the price a company may pay in exercising its IP rights could outweigh the value in doing so. The experience of OneName Inc. is instructive in this respect [see page 111]. Having acquired a patent on a key web technology, OneName became the target of virulent criticism from the web community.

Faced with the potential downside of pursuing its rights, the company felt compelled to re-think its entire commercial attitude. As a consequence, it radically shifted its focus, abandoning the pursuit of royalties in favour of a position that is to all intents and purposes indistinguishable from the open source model.

"What people are finding is that trying to put up a patent in front of the rapidly flowing river of the web is like trying to dam it," points out Drummond Reed, chief technology officer, OneName Inc. "But the river is so powerful that it will simply work around you, or wash over you. We were the first company that said we are not going to contribute intellectual property royalty-free to a W3C standard. And look what happened!"

Copyright owners also have to ask themselves how it would benefit them to be in possession of the world's most powerful encryption technology, and with recourse to the most draconian infringement laws on the planet, if no one were prepared to pay for their content. In addition, what if that content were freely available from other sources on the web? In such a scenario, what advantage does owning IP bestow on them?

With that thought in mind, some IP owners are concluding that the commercial rules of the physical world will never apply on the web. As we have seen, this is a view also propagated by influential web advocates such as John Perry Barlow, and by new economy gurus like Esther Dyson.

As *The New York Times* pointed out on August 6th 2000: "Many internet watchers, Ms. Dyson among them, believe that companies that put information online, from music to books to software, may have to resign themselves to relinquishing control over that material. The fact that you copyrighted something simply may no longer entitle you to control it or get paid for it." What is needed, this line of reasoning argues, is for IP owners to create new business models.

What do you mean: new business model?

What does this signify in practice? Conveniently, the open source movement offers a good model. It is also very successful – with open source software products like Linux and Apache (the most widely used server software on the Internet today) increasingly viewed as a compelling alternative to the traditional proprietary approach exemplified by Microsoft. In fact, argues *CNET* in a special report on open source published in 2000: "Five years from now, it may be impossible to make money charging for operating systems on desktop computers, much less workstations and servers."

But how do companies make money by giving their IP away? Mainly through support selling: open source companies may charge for distribution, or for branding and after-sales service. Alternatively, they may give the software away as a loss-leader, or sell accessories, such as books, compatible hardware, or even complete systems with open source software pre-installed.

Not irrelevant, just different

Interestingly, finding an alternative business model does not mean abandoning IP. It might be used to leverage revenues from other sources – as outlined above. As Dyson puts it: "While content won't be entirely free, the economic dynamics will tend to operate as if it were. Content (including software) will serve as advertising for services such as support, aggregation, filtering, assembly and integration of content modules, or training – or it will be a by-product of paid-for electronic relationships."

IP does not become irrelevant – its role simply changes. It may even be used as a weapon against traditional uses of IP. For instance, Richard Stallman, staunch advocate of the Free Software Foundation (FSF), and originator of the 'copyleft' principle, advises software developers to replace the standard copyright agreement with the FSF's alternative General Public License.

The purpose of this is not in order to seek royalties, but to ensure that free software does not leak back into proprietary systems as a result of competitors incorporating it into their own software, and then copyrighting that. Here, IP becomes a method for ensuring that software remains in the public domain.

OneName demonstrates how this same principle can be applied in the patent arena. "The best model for us is to open it up in this way," says Reed. "The advantage we have is being a first mover. The advantage to everyone is that we will use our intellectual property rights (IPR) very specifically to maintain interoperability. This will neutralise the advantage of much larger companies – such as Microsoft or IBM – who might otherwise try and make it proprietary."

Finding the right note

What about the music industry? While some musicians, such as Metallica and Dr. Dre, have joined with the RIAA and sought to sue Napster, others, like Limp Biskit and The Smashing Pumpkins, have welcomed file-swapping services, with Limp Biskit even organising a concert to support Napster.

More radically, the Offspring announced in September 2000 that they planned to release their next album on the web more than a month before the launch of their CD. In doing so they directly challenged their own record company, Sony.

The band combined this with a novel marketing approach. Fans downloading their latest album can win $1m by registering their email with the band. The aim is to encourage users to then go out and buy the new CD as well, with the enticement that those who do will receive unreleased tracks by email once a month throughout Spring 2001.

Explaining the logic of what they planned, Offspring singer Dexter Holland pointed out, in an *Associated News* story, that although their music was freely downloaded over the web the band's 1998 album had sold nearly 12 million copies in the US. "Digital downloading was not hurting our sales. In fact, it may have been helping."

Eventually it is hoped that viable business models can be achieved by means of a combination of advertising and subscription models. Israeli company, EverAd, for instance, has developed a technology for delivering music file downloads with banner ads attached. And Digital Payloads allows content owners to embed audio advertisements within MP3 files.

Books, too

New approaches are also being adopted by authors. Last year Stephen King made his latest novel, *The Plant,* available for direct download from the web. Payment was based on an honour system, with a recommended price of $1 an instalment. The result was 150,000 downloads during the first week for the first instalment, with some readers voluntarily paying as much as $20 an instalment – in order to ensure that the story continued.

Since then a number of other writers have followed in King's footsteps, including best-selling authors Fay Weldon and Frederick Forsyth. But critics point out that it is one thing for authors or musicians who have already established themselves as powerful brands to adopt such methods, but it is quite another for new entrants.

For traditional publishers and music companies, the concern must be that many of the new approaches are being tested by the content originators themselves. Thus they could find that, in addition to losing royalties, they may be disintermediated – as authors and musicians sell directly to their fans and bypass traditional distribution channels.

Faced with such realities all the major music companies have announced plans to offer new ways of distributing music online. The problem, suggest critics, is that they may still not 'get it'. In October

2000, Universal Music began trials of a new subscription-based service that would offer unlimited access to more than 20,000 songs, at a monthly cost of around $15. It was widely slated because, unlike Napster, Universal's service will not allow subscribers to download the music to their hard disk, but only 'stream' it – which means having to download a large file every time they want to listen to it.

"Users are not getting anything out of this," commented Graham Fisher, an analyst at Bloor Research, to online news service *Silicon.com*. "They would pay for downloadable access or out of print records, but this is like paying to listen to the radio."

However, the fact that Bertelsmann has – in settling with Napster – expressed an interest in investing in the company (as has Universal in its settlement with MP3.com) suggests that music companies may finally be coming to appreciate the need for a radical re-think of their business.

Lawyers will flourish!

So how does the future look? Put simply, it looks likely to be uncertain, litigious and brimming with conflict! The legal profession can expect to flourish and see a busy few years ahead of them. "We see the next five years as being very healthy for consulting and legal professionals who specialise in intellectual property," says Petrash.

The challenge, of course, will lie in keeping up to speed with what is proving to be a very fast-moving area.

Pressure on governments

Governments will face growing pressure from all sides. On the one hand, multinational companies will continue to demand the strengthening and harmonising of global IP laws. This is a development that is likely to be supported by many in the legal profession. "Until a ʂsal set of internet rules is created, we will have to deal with the ʂm of national intellectual property law not fitting the Internet, and thus resulting in legal uncertainties and enforcement problems," points out Mr. Schubert.

On other hand, IP looks set to get caught up in the burgeoning public dissatisfaction over 'corporate-led globalisation', with governments confronted by rising consumer protest over the activities of international institutions like the World Trade Organisation (WTO), which has been at the forefront of initiatives to harmonise and extend IP rights.

The 1999 demonstrations against the WTO in Seattle are now viewed as the starting pistol for an ongoing struggle against globalisation. As *The Economist* pointed out in September 2000, we are already seeing the protesters "prevailing over firms, international institutions and governments partly because, for now, they do reflect that broader mood."

Keen to provide these protests with an intellectual framework, organisations like The International Forum on Globalisation, based in San-Francisco, are right now hammering out a new political agenda of 'global democracy' based on human rights and ecological sustainability. Amongst other things, this includes demands that certain goods and services should not be subject to patents and trade rules.

"There is a train crash coming," says Petrash [see page 23]. "Firstly, there is this perception .... that some countries have an unfair advantage – which may cause these countries to just ignore intellectual property all together. Secondly, there is legal interpretation. For instance, the State Street ruling [allowing business methods to be patented] is only 12 months old, and it takes about 18 months for a patent to get through the system. You can be sure there are thousands of people out there right now writing patents that go beyond State Street that will come in to play in the next two to five years."

· Companies face uncertainty

For companies this means considerable uncertainty over what they will and will not be able to do with their IP in the web economy.

On the one hand it could be argued that the traditional system is successfully asserting itself in cyberspace. Despite the many criticisms, the patenting of software and business methods continues in the US, and is making inroads in Europe. Likewise, ICANN and WIPO initiatives over domain names are clearly helping to extend traditional trademark (and brand) rights into cyberspace. To date, most of the copyright infringement rulings in the US appear to be supporting the traditional interests of the music and entertainment industries.

But these may prove to be pyrrhic victories. In a report published September 2000, Forrester Research predicted that the record industry will lose $3.1bn in potential sales by 2005, in large part because of an increase in illegal file sharing.

Attempts to win the war through the use of the law and Digital Rights Management (DRM) technology, suggested Forrester, will simply send music swapping underground. Already Freenet developers are working on a project called 'Upriser' – which is intended to offer musicians a way to sustain themselves with the proceeds from their music, while maintaining independence from the major labels.

"Traditional publishers must focus on beating Napster at its own game," Forrester analyst Eric Scheirer commented to *E-commerce Times*. "They must create compelling services with the content consumers want, in the formats they want, using the business models they want."

Europe: follower or leader?

Much of the discussion in this book has centred on the US, if only because to date much of debate has taken place in North America and that is where the initial legal battles have been fought. As the discussion and litigation shift to Europe and Asia, we can expect to see political and diplomatic repercussions. Many believe that Europe has an important role to play here.

As Viktor Rainer points out, despite the pressure to allow the patenting of software in Europe, there is currently no appetite for modelling global IP systems around the US system. "I don't think that this would be a good thing, and I don't think it will happen," he says. "In particular, the present generous practice in the US of granting patents on business methods is not welcome in Europe and it does not appear to me that Europe and Japan, intend to follow suit."

Some hope that Europe can act as a counter-balance. "Given that many of these patents will be examined in Europe a year or so after the USPTO I think we may find that that European examiners are able to review them in retrospect, and maybe make decisions that are more appropriate," says Cylink's Chuck Williams.

Europe may also play a stabilising role in the debate over copyright. It is hoped by liberals that one of the major differences between the EU Copyright Directive (still in draft form at the time of writing) will be a more consumer-focused approach. Thus the EU's proposed copyright directive specifies that copyright owners can only use technology to prevent copies provided they have systems in place to allow people who are exempted from the copyright controls to make copies.

Assume the rules may change!

So what can we conclude from all of this? That today there are no certainties.

For those who support the traditional IP system there are some encouraging signs that the traditional model may eventually be migrated to cyberspace. On the other hand, it cannot be denied that the web is proving seriously problematic for traditional IP.

Perhaps the greatest uncertainty today is the extent to which governments may decide to intervene on behalf of consumers. It is governments that ultimately define the rules.

For this reason Petrash cautions IP owners that it would be short-sighted to assume that the rules of today will be the rules of tomorrow; or that the rules of the old economy will be the rules of the new economy. "What the Microsoft [anti-trust] case shows is that the rules can change, and while IP owners may play by all the rules perfectly correctly, they can still lose if they don't have their eyes on the political and social economic trends," he says.

Might we even see governments begin to nationalise IP? Petrash does not rule this out. "We've nationalised major industries before," he says "maybe we will end up with some of this IP becoming very public in the future."

Nevertheless, insists ContentGuard's Ranjit Singh, although IP may be going through a period of transition, no one has yet devised a better system for promoting creativity and innovation. "Sure, the web has created a big chaos for intellectual property," he says, "but if we want to produce new content, and to carry on innovating, people are going to have to be rewarded. If you don't have value for innovation, people won't innovate."

What is not in dispute is that the web poses a number of significant challenges for IP. Challenges that have implications not just for IP owners, but for any company planning to conduct business over the Internet, for the legal system, for governments, and us too – the consumers of IP.

We can expect this debate to continue for some years yet!

**Brian McKenna interviews Lawrence Lessig,
Professor of Law at the Stanford Law School**

Q: Is the web fundamentally different when it comes to IP or is it just a new development that can be absorbed by IP laws?

A: *It raises fundamentally different issues – both the problem of increased risk for IP and the problem of too much protection for IP. A range of new issues in the context of cyberspace will be raised about the relation of IP to free speech and about whether certain kinds of protection for IP, like patents, are needed or helpful. IP lawyers have got to understand that things are different and they must be open to asking fundamental questions.*

Q: You've said that more and stronger IP in a web context will produce more, and richer, lawyers. Should your profession support the growing privatisation of knowledge, or should it lobby governments to call a halt to such privatisation?

A: *It is too much to expect anyone to behave completely altruistically, but at the same time we should advise policy makers to think clearly about how much law we need in this space and advise lawyers to take advantage of what this space offers. It would be foolish of companies not to take advantage of, say, IP protection of patents in cyberspace, but it is a terrible thing that there is such IP protection.*

Q: So, what would you advise a small start-up software house to do? Should it patent whatever it can?

A: *Absolutely, for defensive reasons, because everyone else is. As a lawyer advising a company, I would urge them to take advantage of the system. But as a lawyer thinking about the public policy implications of the matter, I would do what I'm doing – which is to raise questions about whether this propertisation of knowledge makes sense and force the pro-patent lobby to justify what they are doing in terms of public interest, as opposed to the interest of lawyers.*

Q: In your book *Code, and other Laws of Cyberspace*, you speak of law as a direct regulator of social life, but also as something that sits alongside and modifies other means of social regulation – norms, markets, and the built environment of social life. Now, you say that 'cyberspace teaches a new threat to liberty .... [in the form of a] powerful regulator in cyberspace .... this regulator is code'. In a similarly sinister vein you say: 'whatever problems there are when contracts replace copyright, the problems are worse when code displaces copyright law'. What do you mean by code?

A: *I mean the software and hardware that defines cyberspace as it is. A set of computer instructions that constitutes a space, and the experience of it as cyberspace. The architecture that gets built by this hardware and software is the code of cyberspace.*

Q: Your argument is that this code will increasingly replace law as the primary means of defending IP in cyberspace: 'private fences, not public law' is how you put it. What are the implications of that for companies?

A: *I think that they will be keen to find as much private code as they can. They will want this private code to enable more perfect control over the use and distribution of content. And they'll want to do that as quickly as possible before governments figure out that their policies are being displaced by the code that companies are embracing. And so companies will, for instance, invest more in technical staff than in lawyers.*

Q: Is there an irresolvable problem with the practice of trying to rein in an essentially international network, the Internet, using the legal frameworks crafted by nation states?

A: *In my view there is no such thing as what the Internet essentially is. It is hard to rein in cyberspace using national laws, but we are already seeing moves to make it easier by changing its character. I think that's what the course will be, with governments making efforts to facilitate the identification of the country from which someone accesses the web. So France is attempting to require that auction sites treat French citizens differently, and, in the US, there was an injunction against a Canadian company, iCraveTV, that was broadcasting television over the Internet. Another example from the US is internet gambling, so that if you come from a gambling permissive state then that will be allowed and if not then it won't.*

Q: Presumably, this is the kind of thing you mean when you talk, in *Code*, about a kind of citizenship ID in cyberspace? Can you explain this?

A: *Our concept of IDs at the moment is of cards you carry around and produce when the police ask for it. That's not the conception of ID here. In cyberspace IDs are encrypted objects that reside, say, on your computer.*

Q: Do you think cyberspatial IDs constitute the key to resolving the problem of controlling the Internet with national laws?

A: *It's one way that the problem might be solved, and that is one of the reasons why you are going to see a push for it generally. It's about re-establishing national borders in cyberspace.*

Q: It could be said that the US is imposing its intellectual system on the rest of the world through the WTO – through the Trade-Related Aspects of Intellectual Property [TRIPs], for instance. Do you think this is fair?

A: *The thing to remember about the US is that, until 1891, it gave no protection for foreign patents. We were a pirate nation and now we're requiring that everyone follows our IP laws in order to be moral. In general, both those approaches have been mistaken. I would suggest the rest of the world should hesitate before jumping on to the American IP bandwagon. Unfortunately, it looks like Europe will go down the American road of patenting software and business methods, and that will be a terrible thing.*

Q: Is there any possibility that the European Union could shift the
       global agenda and reverse the mounting propertisation of soft-
       ware and business methods? Could Europe convince America
       that patenting software and business methods is simply inadmis-
       sible?

A: *It's conceptually possible, but I see no evidence that European
       governments have the backbone to do that.*

Q: Gordon Petrash of PwC, asked about the forcing of the global IP
       agenda by the US said: "What is wrong with it being led by the
       US? Technology is developing so fast that I think it is good that
       we have a leader that is unrestrained in its look and movement
       to the future." What's your reaction?

A: *There is nothing in principle wrong with having a leader, it's just
       that the US conception is unbalanced. I'd rather have a different
       leader – one that was more balanced, as opposed to one whose
       objective is to maximise IP protection.*

Q: Could WIPO play this role?

A: *That's its function, yes, but I am not confident that WIPO can
       effect progress in these areas because they have got the extreme
       maximising conception too, and that is the problem. I'm
       pessimistic. I don't see that the politics around that will rectify
       the problem. I see a bunch of people who have money one side
       and there is no one on the other side to resist them.*

Q: Do you think that there is an ethical duty for governments to
       take IP into a common space?

A: *I completely think that there is an ethical duty to do that, and
       governments obscure that by making it sound like you promote
       innovation and economic prosperity by expanding IP rights.
       And yet, the fact is that it is both not clear that this kind of
       activity will support innovation. There is a lot of economic
       research that counsels scepticism about that – see, for example,
       the great set of papers at www.researchoninnovation.org. So,*

rather than thinking in a formalistic way – as lawyers are prone to do – about this we ought to think rather more pragmatically, economically really.

Q: The general purpose of this book is to systematically counter-poise two opposing voices – one that says that current IP regimes are, with reform, adequate for cyberspace, and another that says that the nature of the web is such that it changes things radically. How would you situate your own thinking in respect of these two poles?

A: *I embrace both poles. On the one hand, there have been radical changes in the ability to copy and transmit material and those need to be responded to. On the other, there are important tradi-tional values from copyright that we ought to preserve in this space. Those values derive from balance between control by copyright holders and the keeping of material in a commons – by which I mean a resource which people can use without the permission of a third party, or without selective permission of a third party. A park is a commons. Work in the public domain is a commons. A highway is a commons. They are all spaces of important freedom from the control of others. This is important for creativity and 'fair use' because sometimes progress is in a direction that those in control now don't much like. I might want to criticise you by using your song; I might want to develop an operating system in a way that is inconsistent with your busi-ness model for operating systems. The key to that innovation is keeping a large part of the space here 'free' – free from control by government, and private forces.*

Brian Mckenna interviews Mark Stefik, Manager of the Information Sciences Laboratory, Xerox Palo Alto Research Center

Q: Does the Internet create a fundamentally different terrain for IP?

A: *It does and I'd pose the question of what it is different from, namely paper. If you compare a paper publisher with a digital publisher the danger to copyright is much greater. If you used a copying machine to reproduce books it would cost you more than the publisher. That's just not true of digital works.*

Q: Lawrence Lessig admits to the increased threat to copyright holders posed by digital copying, but suggests that publishers may accrue too much power through proprietary computer code. You've been involved in the development of just such code, in the form of Xerox's ContentGuard.

A: *Lessig is right that this could be misused and publishers get too much power. Publishers and readers are part of a larger system that will tend to adjust, so that if the publishers abuse power it won't serve them well. The whole social system has to look again at things like 'fair use'. An argument that I have made with Alex Silverman – in our paper* The Bit and the Pendulum – *is that we need to revisit 'fair use' with an eye to what differentiates the network from previous media. Publishers may try to get more power by the way their codes are written, but a pirate can do much greater damage than with paper.*

To address 'fair use' we have to look at all the risks and benefits in it, which is why Alex Silverman and I promote the idea that 'fair use', rather than being treated as a legal defence against infringement, should be subject to control, like a driver's licence.

Q: Can you expand on this notion?

A: *Everybody would get a certain amount of usage on any contract, but some people could get greater use if they showed knowledge of what the laws are by possession of a licence. And if they misuse their 'fair use' privilege their accountability should be backed up by an insurance fund to which all stakeholders would contribute.*

When Lessig makes his arguments about publishers having too much power he is not open to the possibility of adjusting the ways in which the laws work. He wants to keep 'fair use' as a legal defence, but you can get much of the effect of 'fair use' if there is a 'fair use' license.

Q: How do you think the US compares with Europe on IP and the Internet? Should European software companies follow the American route of patenting as much as possible?

A: *I don't think the US is settled about how well the patent system is working, either. The US patent examiners do not have an adequate background, so there have been a lot of patents awarded that shouldn't have been. In some ways, the European patenting system is better – it's quicker, there's public comment before patents are issued. So I wouldn't make the argument that the US system is better and everyone else should adopt it.*

Q: What's your view on the Napster case?

A: *The Napster controversy is a symptom of a phenomenon I call 'the Internet Edge' – the 'edge' in psychology is what a person goes through when on the verge of a life-changing experience. In psycho-dynamics you often see 'edge behaviour' – when someone steps into a change, becomes frightened by it, backs up, then moves forward again. The thesis of my book* The Internet Edge: Social, Technical and Legal Challenges for a Networked World (1999) *is that we are in the middle of collective edge behaviour. So I see Napster et al making a move in a certain direction and then a push back from another part of the economy saying 'we're not ready for this'. The hooplah won't die down until we've figured out how to balance the interests of all the stakeholders.*

Q: Maybe the Napsters of this world cannot be stopped and business models have to adjust to the reality of mass copyright infringement on the Internet?

A: *We haven't seen anything like what the digital arms race could become. Napster is a skirmish by kids. If companies really wanted to shut down Napster they could do it with a denial of service attack, they could send out viruses to wipe out Napster. No one is playing that kind of hardball yet. It's not true that these people cannot be stopped. People believe they can't because of the softball that's been played. You could go one step beyond Napster et al and encrypt stuff.*

Q: What do you see as the future?

A: *We want a situation where there is enormous convenience for the consumers. The reason there is so much energy fuelling phenomena like Napster is that digital works cost too much. And people don't want to pay the big distribution overhead. You still need to pay the creators, but the idea that you have to pay so much for printing plastic and bricks-and-mortar means of distribution isn't valid. If you have reasonably priced digital works, and convenient ways of getting them, then this bootlegging will go away.*

In five years the two current models of buying a CD from a store or downloading music from the Internet to a PC will be irrelevant. Instead there will be convenient, let's say voice-activated, distribution to a variety of devices (for example your car), lots of personalisation, and subscription-based services where the music will find you. You won't have to fiddle around with bootlegging software.

Q: You believe that people currently infringe copyright because there is no convenient means of paying for digital content?

A: *That's true for the vast majority of people, yes.*

Q: And you believe that the way forward for media companies is not to join the Napsters by evolving business models based on free content, but that trusted systems offer a better way?

A: *There will be niches. In many cases people will accept advertising as a way of paying. In others there won't be enough mass appeal and there will have to be some money exchange mechanism. Another possible model is the 'sponsored browser', where the advertiser will pay the fees if you watch enough ads. A few years ago Esther Dyson said the way to do it was to distribute content free and build services around that, but she was modelling the world after herself.*

Q: Where are we with trusted system technology?

A: *Most of the distribution has been on PCs and they are simply not secure enough, but we are starting to see the introduction of electronic books, which are more secure. Of course there is the DVD fiasco with the Decode Content Scrambling System (DeCSS) case where the anti-copyright technology was circumvented. The vendors didn't understand security to a professional enough level.*

Q: Politically, aren't governments backing up the IP rights of big corporations against web users?

A: *Politicians go with the flow. And there are governments, for example the Chinese, who don't want any IP protection at all.*

   The international aspects are interesting, and code is particularly important since it runs the same in any country. The net goes everywhere. Right now we don't have the speed bumps of national boundaries. Think about the tax implications of that. Suppose you are from the US, you are travelling in France and you download software over the net from the US. Have you imported or exported it? You come back to the US through customs. Again, are you importing or exporting?

Alex Silverman and I have proposed a solution. We ought to register computers like we register ships. If you have a British computer downloading US software then, no matter where it is, you know whether you are importing or exporting and can answer the question of whether there should be any taxation. This is just one example of the problems around nationality thrown up by our virtual world.

Biographies

Richard Poynder is a freelance writer who specialises in internet technologies, the electronic information industry and intellectual property issues. A former editor of *Information World Review,* Richard writes for a wide range of information industry publications, and contributes regularly to the *London Financial Times.* He is also commissioning editor, and co-author, of *Hidden Value, The Derwent Guide to Managing Intellectual Property.* Contact: www.richardpoynder.com

Hugh Brett is editor of the *European Intellectual Property Review*, and of Counsel with the international law firm of White & Case. He is a Professorial Fellow at Queen Mary & Westfield College, London University.

Paul Gosling is a journalist and author, specialising in IT, finance and the public sector. He has written for *The Independent, Independent on Sunday, Sunday Times, Express* and *Mail on Sunday* and many leading magazines. His books include *Changing Money* and *Government in the Digital Age*, as well as being co-author of Derwent's *Hidden Value: The Derwent Guide to Managing Intellectual Property.* Contact: paulgosling@email.msn.com

Brian McKenna is a business editor at *VNU Business Online UK.* He is a former managing editor of *Online Information Review* and *The Electronic Library*, and former editor of *Knowledge Management* and *Information World Review.* Contact: brian_mckenna@vnu.co.uk

Further reading

Code and Other Laws of Cyberspace by Lawrence Lessig, Basic Books, 2000

Owning the Future by Seth Shulman, Houghton Mifflin Company, 1999

Rembrandts in the Attic by Kevin Rivette and David Kline, Harvard Business School Press, 1999

The Patent Wars by Fred Warshofsky, John Wiley & Sons, 1994

Weaving the Web by Tim Berners-Lee, TEXERE Publishing, 2000

Index

1-Click: 1, 9, 10, 100, 104, 114, 154
2600: 2, 16, 43, 48, 60, 134

A
Aharonian, Greg: 102, 104
Amazon.com: 10, 100, 101, 154
Anti-Cybersquatting Consumer Protection Act: 70
AOL: 41, 44, 45, 133
Article 52: 104, 106, 160
Association of American Publishers: 125, 132

B
bad faith: 70, 75, 77, 79, 84, 85, 90
Bayh-Dole Act: 95
Bertelsmann: 2, 166
Bezos, Jeff: 2, 9, 12, 100, 101
Boucher, Rick: 158, 159
Brimelow, Alison: 160
British Phonographic Institute: 35, 53
British Telecom: 10, 21
BT: See *British Telecom*
Business Method Patent Improvement Act: 159
Business Software Alliance, The: 36

C
CAFC: See *Court of Appeals of the Federal Circuit*
Chartered Institute of Patent Agents: 13, 22, 105, 160
Chiariglione, Leonardo: 135, 140
CIPA: See *Chartered Institute of Patent Agents*
Code and Other Laws of Cyberspace: 8, 138, 155
ContentGuard: 14, 129, 130, 131, 170, 176
copy-duty: 138

WAP: See *Wireless Application Protocol*
Warshofsky, Fred: 7, 12, 95, 96
watermarks: 14, 24, 99, 125, 127-128, 130, 131-132, 134, 141, 142
WIPO: See World Intellectual Property Organisation
WIPO Copyright Treaty: ix, 13, 34, 46
WIPO Performances and Phonograms Treaty: ix, 13, 34
Wireless Application Protocol: 10
World Intellectual Property Organisation: 11, 13, 16, 33, 34, 35, 46, 50, 52, 74, 75, 76, 77, 78, 79, 81, 84, 85, 90, 105, 153, 168, 174
World Trade Organisation: 14, 17, 104, 105, 167, 173
World Wide Web Consortium: 6, 111, 112, 162
WTO: See *World Trade Organisation*

X
Xerox: 14, 176
XrML: See *eXtensible rights Markup Language*

Y
Yeates, Andrew: 53